INTERNET EXPLORER 6
in easy steps

GW00600802

MARY LOJKINE

COMPUTER
STEP

In easy steps is an imprint of Computer Step
Southfield Road . Southam
Warwickshire CV47 0FB . England

http://www.ineasysteps.com

Notice of Liability

Every effort has been made to ensure that this book contains accurate
and current information. However, Computer Step and the author
shall not be liable for any loss or damage suffered by readers as a
result of any information contained herein.

Trademarks

Microsoft® and Windows® are registered trademarks of Microsoft
Corporation. All other trademarks are acknowledged as belonging to
their respective companies.

Printed and bound in the United Kingdom

ISBN 1-84078-147-5

Table of Contents

Exploring the web   73

4

Intermediate browsing   105

5

Usenet newsgroups   173

9

Index   187

Getting started

Before you can use Internet Explorer, you need to get connected to the Internet. This chapter explains what that means and outlines your options. It then shows you how to obtain, install and run Internet Explorer.

Covers

Chapter One

Introduction to the Internet

This book is in three sections. Chapters 1–4 cover the things you need to know to start using Internet Explorer. Chapters 5–7 cover more advanced features. Chapters 8–9 explain how to use Outlook Express, the e-mail and news program supplied with Internet Explorer.

The Internet is a 'network of networks' that connects computers from all around the world. It's estimated that over 100 million people use the Internet, and the number increases every day.

You can use the Internet to access the latest news; research almost any topic you can imagine; shop for products and services; or get information about your favourite sport or pastime. You can also send messages to your friends, participate in discussion groups and obtain software for your computer.

History of the Internet

The Internet has its roots in 1969, when the US Government decided to connect some of its computers together so scientists and military agencies could communicate more easily. The system was designed to be very robust, so there was no control centre. Each machine operated independently and messages travelled by whatever route seemed most convenient at the time. Even if some of the computers were destroyed by a military or terrorist attack, the others could carry on exchanging information.

In the 1970s several more computer networks were established by military and academic institutions. Eventually many of these networks were linked together, creating the network of networks we now know as 'the Internet'. During the 1980s the Internet was dominated by scientists, academics, computer experts and students, but the user-friendly software of the 1990s has encouraged a much wider range of people to make use of it. By the end of the 2000s you'll be taking it for granted.

Although some parts of the world are better represented than others, the Internet is a truly global phenomenon. You can connect to a computer in Australia or New Zealand as easily – and as cheaply – as to one just down the road.

No-one owns or controls the Internet, although there are various organisations that endeavour to keep everything running smoothly. It can be creaky, cranky and intensely irritating, but for the most part it works remarkably well.

The World Wide Web is not the same thing as the Internet. The Internet is a network of computers. The web is a service that uses the Internet to transfer information from one place to another. Other services include e-mail (Chapter 8) and newsgroups (Chapter 9).

Turn to Chapter 4 for more information about some of the most popular pages on the web.

The World Wide Web

The recent surge of interest in the Internet is due to the World Wide Web. Developed in 1990 at CERN, the European Laboratory for Particle Physics, the web consists of millions of magazine-style pages. Unlike pages in a printed magazine, however, web pages can include sound samples, animations, video clips and interactive elements as well as text and pictures.

Web pages are connected together by 'hypertext' links – electronic cross references that enable you to jump from page to page by clicking on underlined text or highlighted images. A page stored on a computer in London might have links to pages stored in Moscow, Tokyo and Washington, which in turn might be linked to pages in many other countries. The result is a network of connections stretching right around the globe – hence 'World Wide Web'.

You don't need to know where any of the pages are, because you can follow the links. However, if you know the address of the page you want to view, you can jump straight to it.

Anyone can create a web page, so there's a huge range of material to explore. Government departments, museums and educational institutions are pouring information on to the web, and many companies use it to promote their products or sell directly to the public. Publishers and broadcasters produce on-line magazines and news services, and you'll find many pages dedicated to the hobbies and interests of private individuals.

Web browsers

In order to look at – or 'browse' – web pages, you need a piece of software called a 'web browser'. It enables you to find web pages and display them on your computer's screen.

Internet Explorer is Microsoft's web browser. It's a good choice for beginners because it's free and easy to use. It comes with a companion program called Outlook Express that enables you to send messages and join discussions.

Connecting to the Internet

Before you can access the web, you need to be connected to the Internet. There are four possibilities: your company or university may provide a direct connection; you can visit a cyber café or public library; you can use a modem (a device that enables computers to communicate with each other over a phone line); or you can sign up for a high-speed 'broadband' connection.

Company connections

The rest of this chapter assumes you're using a modem to connect to the Internet. If you are connecting via a university or company network, ask your systems manager to help you install and configure Internet Explorer.

If you are at university, or work for a large company that has an internal computer network, you may already be connected to the Internet. Ask your systems manager if it's possible to access the World Wide Web from your PC, Macintosh or workstation.

The advantage of a company connection is that you don't have to pay for it. However, you have to be at work to access the Internet and there may be rules about what you can use it for.

Cyber cafés, pubs and libraries

The cyber café is the Internet equivalent of the public telephone, although it's generally warmer and more comfortable. You can drink coffee (or beer, in a cyber pub) and use the café's computers to access the Internet. Most charge by the half hour or hour, and the rates are quite reasonable. Your local library may also have computers you can use.

If you aren't sure whether the Internet is for you, paying to use someone else's equipment for a few hours is a good way to find out. You don't have to worry about setting up the software and there's usually someone to help with any problems. However, you may not have access to the full range of Internet services – for example, you may not be able to send and receive e-mail.

Dial-up connections

The most versatile option is to use a modem to connect your home computer to the Internet. Regrettably, this is also the option that requires the most input – both financial and technical – from you.

You need five things to establish a dial-up connection:

1   A computer. Internet Explorer is available for several types of computer, but this book concentrates on the version for PCs running Windows. At the very least, you'll need a PC with a

Internet Explorer 6 does not work with Windows 95. It requires Windows 98, 98SE, Millennium Edition (Me), XP, NT 4.0 or 2000.

V.90 modems don't actually run at 56kbps – that's their theoretical top speed. In reality, they operate at 45–50kbps.

486 processor running at 66MHz, 16Mb of RAM (32Mb for Windows Me, NT 4.0 or 2000) and 25 to 75Mb of free hard-disk space. A faster, more powerful computer with more RAM will make web browsing more enjoyable.

2 A modem. Most new computers have an internal modem. If you need to buy a modem, an external model that connects to one of the sockets on the back of your PC is easier to install. Make sure it conforms to the V.90 standard, giving it a top speed of 56kbps (kilobits per second).

3 A telephone line. You'll be making a phone call, usually at the local rate, each time you connect.

4 An Internet Service Provider, or ISP (see overleaf). A Service Provider has a computer system that is permanently connected to the Internet, and to a bank of modems. You use your modem to connect to one of your service provider's modems, via your telephone line, thereby making your computer (temporarily) part of the Internet.

5 Connection software (see page 15). You'll find the Dial-Up Networking utility on your Windows CD.

Broadband connections

The technology used to provide high-speed connections over a regular telephone line is called 'Asymmetric Digital Subscriber Line', or 'ADSL' for short.

If you intend to use the Internet a lot, you may want a faster connection that doesn't tie up your phone line. Broadband services use special modems to transmit data over the cable television or telephone networks, without affecting your ability to watch TV or make voice calls. Most services are at least ten times as fast as regular dial-up connections.

You are charged a flat monthly rate, so broadband services are good value if you use the Internet for several hours each day. If you're a light to moderate user, a dial-up connection will be cheaper.

For cable-based services, contact the cable television company that serves your area. High-speed services that operate over regular telephone lines are available through Internet Service Providers.

Internet Service Providers

An Internet Service Provider (ISP) enables you to connect to the Internet via a modem and telephone line. Most ISPs also provide basic software and have technical-support people who can help with any problems.

Free services

ISPs such as Freeserve and Virgin Net, offer 'free' services – it costs nothing to open an account and there is no monthly fee. However, that doesn't mean you get free access to the Internet. Each time you connect, you're making a telephone call, so you'll notice an increase in your phone bill.

These ISPs fund their services in two ways. First, they get a percentage of your call charges. You don't pay any extra for your calls, but your phone company makes a bit less, because it passes on some of the money to the service provider. Second, if you have problems and need to call the technical-support line, you are charged a premium rate – typically 50p or £1 per minute.

Free services offer a good deal for people who are reasonably comfortable with computers. If you think you'll need help installing and running your Internet software, you might be better off with a subscription-based service.

Subscription-based services

Some services offer one-month free trials for new users. They're a good way to find out what you'll get for your money. If you decide not to continue, ring up and close your account before the trial ends. If you don't, you'll be liable for the monthly fees.

'Regular' ISPs such as Demon Internet and PIPEX charge a monthly fee for their services. This arrangement used to be the norm and still has some advantages. First, subscription-based ISPs offer technical support on local-rate numbers, so you can sort out problems without running up an enormous phone bill. Second, they have more money to invest in infrastructure, so you get a more reliable service. With free services, you may have problems during peak hours. You might have difficulty connecting because all the lines are engaged, or find that everything gets very slow.

Some regular ISPs offer additional services such as e-mail addresses for all the family, access to a games server, global roaming so you can access the Net while you're overseas, and reception or forwarding of faxes. They may also offer broadband services (see previous page), enabling you to upgrade to a faster connection as your Internet use increases.

On-line services

The third option is to join an on-line service such as AOL or CompuServe. On-line services are similar to regular ISPs, but also have subscriber-only content and private discussion forums. This was a big plus in the days when there weren't many reliable news services on the web, and business users may still find they offer information that isn't available elsewhere. They also enable parents to provide restricted Internet access for their children.

The other difference is that each on-line service has its own software. They all give you a customised version of Internet Explorer for browsing the web, but may have special software for connecting to the Internet and sending e-mail messages. Free and subscription-based ISPs let you use whatever software you fancy and are a better choice if you want to experiment with different programs.

Choosing an ISP

Once you've decided what type of service provider you require, you need to settle on a particular service. Most Internet magazines publish lists you can refer to. The things to consider are:

1   Level of service. Make sure you'll be getting full Internet access, including e-mail, newsgroups and the web. Find out what software is supplied, especially if you're considering an on-line service, and whether you can use something else if you don't like it. If you're planning to create your own web pages, ask about free web space.

2   Access numbers. Most service providers use special phone numbers that are charged at the same rate as a local call, no matter where you call from. Some offer special deals that reduce the cost of your phone calls (see overleaf).

3   Modem speed. Make sure your service provider supports the fastest speed your modem can manage.

4   Subscriber-to-modem ratio. If you choose a service provider that has a lot more subscribers than modems, you'll find it hard to get through. Aim for a ratio of around 15 subscribers per modem (15:1).

5   Broadband services. You may only want a regular connection at the moment, but you might need something faster in the future. Find out whether you'll be able to upgrade to a high-speed cable or ADSL service.

6   Technical support. Find out how much you'll be charged for calls to the helpline, and check the opening hours – a helpline that is only available during the day won't be much good if you're expecting to use the Internet after work or at the weekend. If you don't have much experience with computers, call up and ask a few questions. If the person on the other end can't answer them clearly, try another ISP.

Call charges

Whichever type of service provider you choose, you can run up significant telephone bills, especially if you use the Internet during the day. Over the last couple of years phone companies and service providers have introduced all sorts of schemes that aim to reduce the overall cost. Some offer lower rates, some give you free calls in the evenings and at weekends, and others let you use the Internet as much as you want for a fixed monthly charge.

Schemes come and go so quickly that it's impossible to make any recommendations. If a deal sounds too good to be true, it probably is – even if it is being trumpeted in the national press. Read all the small print very carefully before you commit yourself. If you have to change phone companies, check the cost of ordinary (voice) calls, make sure you'll get all the services you need, and find out whether you're locked in for a minimum period of time.

Most of the schemes are aimed at people who use the Internet for many hours each week. If you are a light user and can confine your sessions to off-peak periods (evenings and weekends), you won't need to remortgage your house to pay your phone bill. Work out how much you're actually spending on phone calls before you sign up for any of these deals – they won't necessarily save you money.

Dial-Up Networking

These days getting on to the Internet just involves installing your service provider's software pack. You don't need to understand how the connection software works, and you can skip to page 17 if you aren't interested.

Establishing a connection

Before you can use Internet Explorer, or any other Internet application, you need to persuade your modem to connect your computer to the Internet. You do this by running a small program called Dial-Up Networking, which stores your service provider's details and controls your modem.

As well as sorting out the connection, Dial-Up Networking establishes a TCP/IP interface, enabling other programs to send and receive data. TCP/IP stands for Transmission Control Protocol/Internet Protocol and it's the common language of the Internet. Many different computers can run TCP/IP software, so everyone can join in.

How the Internet works

Every computer on the Internet has a unique address, or 'IP number', which looks something like 194.164.95.33 Many computers also have names, such as www.ineasysteps.com The Domain Name System (DNS) converts the easy-to-remember names into computer-friendly numbers when you type in an address.

TCP and IP are responsible for getting data from one address to another. TCP breaks it up into small 'packets' and adds the address, then IP gets the packets to their destination, using any available route. At the other end, TCP checks that all the packets have arrived and reassembles them in the correct order.

If there's a problem somewhere along the way, the packets are rerouted to avoid it. They might not all take the same route, and some packets go missing and have to be re-sent, but everything should get there in the end – without any help from you. What you will notice is that packets don't arrive in a steady stream. You often get a bunch of packets, and then a gap, and then another bunch, and so on.

...cont'd

If you need to install Dial-Up Networking yourself, click the Start button and go to Settings > Control Panel. Double-click the Add/Remove Programs icon, click the Windows Setup tab and look for Dial-Up Networking in the Components list – it should be under Communications. Select it, click OK twice and follow the on-screen instructions.

Installing and using Dial-Up Networking

Your service provider's setup disk will check whether Dial-Up Networking is installed on your PC. If it isn't, it will ask you to insert your Windows CD so it can install it for you.

1   To open Dial-Up Networking, click the Start button and select Programs>Accessories>Communications. You should see a Make New Connection icon and an icon for your service provider

2   To add an icon for another service provider, double-click Make New Connection and follow the on-screen instructions. Alternatively, run the Internet Connection Wizard – see page 21

Dial-Up Networking is often shortened to 'DUN' and you may see the service provider icons referred to as 'DUN connectoids.'

3   To connect to your service provider manually, double-click its icon (normally Internet Explorer will do this automatically)

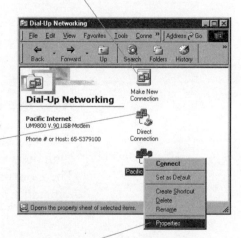

4   If your service provider's phone number changes or you buy a new modem, right-click your service provider's icon and select Properties to enter the new details

Obtaining Internet Explorer

Most service providers include a copy of Internet Explorer in their start-up package. It's also included with software products such as Microsoft Office and you'll often find it on the CDs attached to computer magazines. If you've only just bought your PC, you'll probably find it has been preinstalled by the manufacturer. Failing all that, you can order Internet Explorer directly from Microsoft.

'Download' means to copy a file from a computer on the Internet to your computer. 'Uploading' a file copies it from your computer to one on the Internet.

If you're already an Internet user, you can download Internet Explorer from Microsoft's web site. You'll need plenty of patience, though – a 'typical' installation can take over an hour to download.

1 Connect to Microsoft's web site at:

`http://www.microsoft.com/windows/ie/`

2 This page changes regularly, but it's always linked to the download area. Look for a 'Download Now' button or heading. Click it to go to the download pages

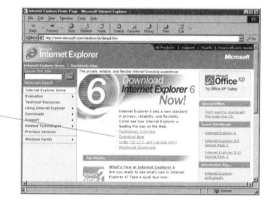

3 Follow Microsoft's on-screen instructions to download the Internet Explorer setup program

4 When the setup program has been copied on to your hard disk, follow the instructions on pages 18–20. When you get to Step 13, the setup program will download the rest of the Internet Explorer files and install them for you

Installing Internet Explorer

If you're installing Internet Explorer from a disk supplied by your service provider, follow whatever instructions have been provided. They will include details of any service-specific settings or options.

If you're installing Internet Explorer from a magazine's cover-mounted CD, or have ordered a CD from Microsoft, you'll get a menu screen when you insert the disk. Look for an 'Install Internet Explorer 6' option and click it to start the setup program.

If you are using a service provider's setup disk, some screens may look slightly different, and there may be extra steps where you're prompted to enter personal details such as your name and preferred e-mail address.

1 The Wizard helps you install Internet Explorer. Click here to accept the licence agreement

2 Click Next to proceed

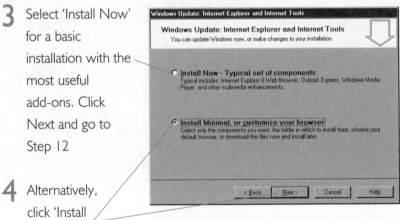

3 Select 'Install Now' for a basic installation with the most useful add-ons. Click Next and go to Step 12

4 Alternatively, click 'Install Minimal, or customize…' to decide which components should be installed. Click Next and go to Step 5

...cont'd

Not sure what a component does? Click on its name to select it and a brief description appears on the right.

5 Select Minimal, Typical or Full as a starting point

6 Click the checkboxes to add or remove components

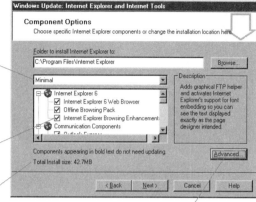

Some items may already be installed on your PC. If so, their names are shown in bold. You don't need to install them again.

7 The amount of hard-disk space required is shown here

8 Click Advanced for two more options

9 This option is for people who have several web browsing programs

Selecting the 'Download only' option means you have a backup of the installation files on your hard disk and can reinstall Internet Explorer 6 without downloading them again.

10 This option will be available if you're downloading Internet Explorer (see page 17). Select it to copy the files on to your hard disk instead of installing the program straightaway

11 Click OK to go back to the screen shown in Step 5, then click Next to proceed

12 Follow the additional steps overleaf

If you are downloading Internet Explorer, the setup program automatically connects to the Internet and fetches all the files.

13 Wait while the setup program installs all the components you've selected. It takes several minutes to install Internet Explorer

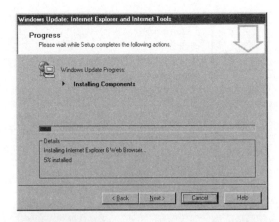

14 When you see this screen, click Finish to restart your computer

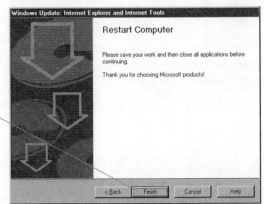

If you have been using an earlier version of Internet Explorer, your icon will be in the same place as before. However, it will now run Internet Explorer 6.

15 When your computer restarts, you'll have an Internet Explorer icon on your desktop:

Internet
Explorer

Internet Connection Wizard

The Internet Connection Wizard makes it easy to enter the details of your Internet account. If you're using a service provider's setup disk, you won't need to run the Wizard (although some of its screens may pop up during the installation process) and you can skip to page 23. The Wizard is useful if you have to set up an account manually, perhaps because you've bought a new computer and can't find your old setup disk.

You will need to know: your service provider's phone number (the modem number, not the one you call to talk to someone); your user name and password, your e-mail address, and the addresses of your service provider's mail servers. Your service provider will give you these details.

You can also run the Wizard from Internet Explorer. Go to Tools> Internet Options and click the Connections tab, then click Setup.

1 Go to the Start menu and choose Programs>Accessories> Communications>Internet Connection Wizard. Answer the questions, clicking Next after each step

2 Select the third option then Next

3 Select 'I connect through a phone line and modem' then Next

4 Enter the phone number you use to connect to your service provider then click Next

5 Enter your user name and password

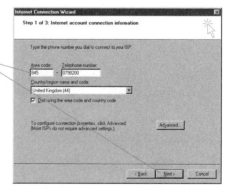

6 Enter a name for the connection. The name of your service provider will do nicely

7 You'll be prompted to set up your e-mail account

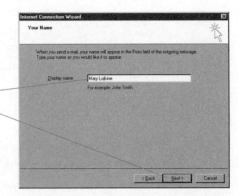

8 Enter your name

9 Enter your e-mail address and click Next

10 Unless you've been told otherwise, set the server type to POP3. Enter the addresses of your service provider's mail servers

11 Enter your user name and password. Usually these will be the same as before, but some service providers give you different ones for e-mail

12 Click Finish – that's all there is to it!

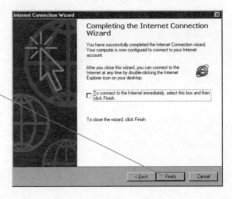

Running Internet Explorer

To run Internet Explorer, double-click its icon or select it from the Programs section of the Start menu.

Internet Explorer

Opening a connection to the Internet is often referred to as 'logging on.' Likewise, 'logging off' means closing the connection.

1 If your computer isn't set up to connect to the Internet, the Internet Connection Wizard will run – see page 21

2 Most service providers' setup discs sort out the connection for you, so you're more likely to see a log-on screen

3 Enter your user name and password

If you tell your computer to save your password, anyone with access to it can connect to the Internet.

4 If you want your computer to remember your password, select this checkbox

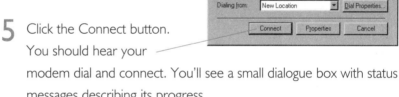

If you select 'Connect automatically', you won't need to click the Connect button in future.

5 Click the Connect button. You should hear your modem dial and connect. You'll see a small dialogue box with status messages describing its progress

6 Internet Explorer displays a web page like this, or possibly a page from your service provider's web site

7 Now you can go to Chapter 2 and learn how to browse the web. To disconnect, see overleaf

The System Tray is a sunken area at the right-hand end of the Windows Taskbar.

8 When you close Internet Explorer, you'll be prompted to close the connection. Click Disconnect Now to log off

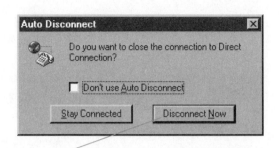

9 To disconnect without closing Internet Explorer, go to the System Tray and look for an icon showing two computers connected together. Double-click it

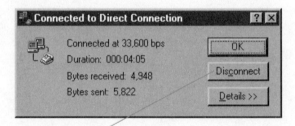

10 Click the Disconnect button to log off

Fine-tuning your connection

Your connection settings determine how and when Internet Explorer connects to the Internet. You can alter them to make sure it only connects when you want it to, and disconnects automatically when the connection is idle.

You can change your settings from Control Panel, too. Double-click the Internet Options icon to access the dialogue box shown here.

| Go to Internet Explorer's Tools menu and select Internet Options. Click the Connections tab

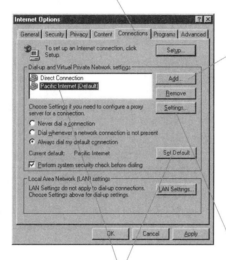

2 Click Add to enter Dial-Up Networking settings (see page 15) for a second service provider

3 Select 'Never dial...' to make connections manually using Dial-Up Networking. 'Always dial...' enables Internet Explorer to make connections as required and is the best choice

To use a connection other than the default one, select it from the drop-down list at the top of the log-on screen (see page 23) before you click Connect.

4 If you have accounts with several service providers, all the possible connections are listed here. Tell Internet Explorer which one to use by selecting it and clicking Set Default

5 To fine-tune a connection, select it and click Settings. This opens the dialogue box shown overleaf

...cont'd

A proxy server stores copies of all the web pages that have been viewed by people who use your service provider. If there's a copy of the page you want to see, Internet Explorer can download it from the proxy server more quickly than it could fetch it from the original web site.

6 If your service provider has a proxy server, enter the details here

7 If your user name or password changes, update your details here

8 Click Properties to check your service provider's phone number and make sure your modem details are correct.

9 Click the Dialing tab

10 If all your service provider's modems are busy, Internet Explorer will redial. Specify how many times it should try and how long it should wait between attempts

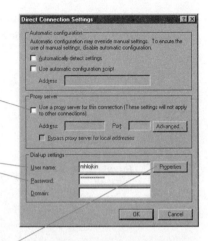

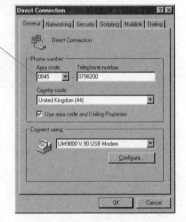

If you enable both the 'Disconnect' options, you won't run up a big phone bill if you get distracted and forget to log off. Internet Explorer will automatically terminate the connection.

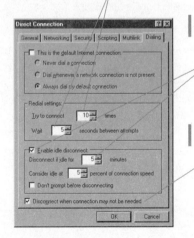

11 Select 'Enable idle disconnect' to drop the line if you don't seem to be doing anything. You may want to reduce the idle time

12 Select 'Disconnect when connection may not be needed' to end your session if you've closed all your Internet programs

Basic web browsing

This chapter shows you how to enter web addresses and jump from page to page. It also explains what to do when you come across images, sounds, video clips and program files. Finally, you'll learn how to save and print web pages.

Covers

Chapter Two

Introducing Internet Explorer

Like most Windows programs, Internet Explorer has a title bar, menu bar and toolbars across the top of the window, and a status bar at the bottom. The most important areas of the screen are:

Service Providers sometimes customise Internet Explorer, so your version may look slightly different.

Title bar – displays the name of the page

Menu bar

Standard buttons

Address bar – displays the address, or URL, of the page

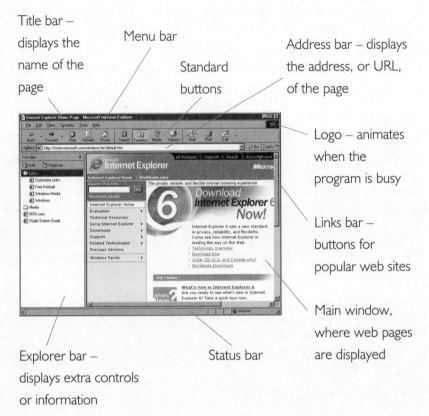

Logo – animates when the program is busy

Links bar – buttons for popular web sites

Main window, where web pages are displayed

Explorer bar – displays extra controls or information

Status bar

Customising the toolbars

You can rearrange the Menu bar, Standard buttons, Address bar and Links bar, or turn off some of the bars to increase the size of the main window.

You can also turn toolbars on or off from View>Toolbars.

1 To turn off a toolbar, right-click on an empty section. A pop-up menu appears. Deselect the toolbar you no longer wish to display

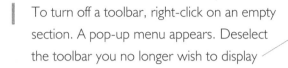

The toolbars have to be at the top of the window. You can't move them to the side or the bottom, or turn them into floating tool palettes.

2 To move a toolbar, use your mouse to grab the grey handle at the left-hand end. Drag it up, down or across

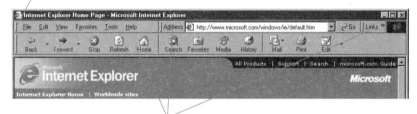

3 You can have several toolbars on the same line

Another way to increase the screen area is by selecting View>Full Screen. If this mode is too minimalist for you, right-click on the Standard buttons to add some of the other toolbars.

4 To expand a toolbar, double-click on its handle. Double-click again to expand it further, and a third time to put it away

5 If Internet Explorer doesn't have enough space to display all the buttons on a toolbar, it adds an arrow button ➤ at the right-hand end. Click on it to access the missing buttons

6 If you find you're moving the toolbars by accident, right-click on an empty section and select Lock the Toolbars

Customising the Standard Buttons

As you become more experienced, you may want to change the Standard buttons. You can add buttons for more advanced features or remove the button for features you don't use. You can also turn off the text labels and reduce the size of the buttons to create a more compact toolbar.

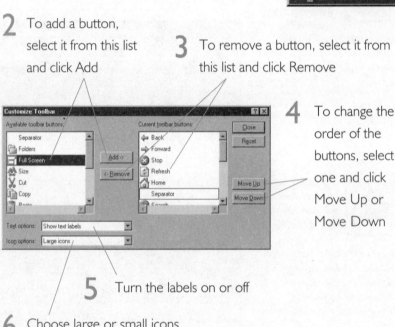

1 To customise the Standard buttons, right-click on an empty section of the toolbar. Select Customize

Separators are grey lines that can be used to divide the toolbar into sections. Add as many as you need to keep your toolbar tidy.

2 To add a button, select it from this list and click Add

3 To remove a button, select it from this list and click Remove

4 To change the order of the buttons, select one and click Move Up or Move Down

5 Turn the labels on or off

If you select 'No text labels' and 'Small icons', your toolbar will look like the toolbars in Microsoft Office.

6 Choose large or small icons

7 Click Close to finish, or Reset to undo all your changes

Understanding addresses

Chapter 4 contains a selection of addresses for you to try.

Once you're comfortable with the interface, you're ready to go somewhere. Every page on the web has a unique address, otherwise known as a Uniform Resource Locator (URL). You've probably seen some web addresses in newspapers and magazines and on television.

The URL for Microsoft's Internet Explorer web page is:

A page is a single web document. Some are quite long – use the scroll bar to move down them. A site is a collection of related pages, and the server is the computer on which all the documents are stored.

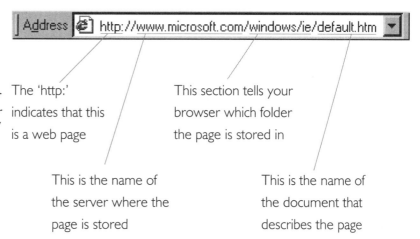

The 'http:' indicates that this is a web page

This section tells your browser which folder the page is stored in

This is the name of the server where the page is stored

This is the name of the document that describes the page

Internet Explorer assumes you are looking for a web page, so you don't have to type the `http://` at the beginning. If you're looking for the main page of a company's site, you can also leave out everything after the first single slash. To find the main page of Microsoft's web site, you would enter: `www.microsoft.com`

Decoding server names

Most server names have three or four sections:

You don't have to know how to interpret a server name – you just have to type it correctly. However, if you know how the names are constructed, you can spot mistakes and work out how to fix them.

```
www.microsoft.com
www.bbc.co.uk
```

The last section (`.com`) or last two sections (`.co.uk`) tell you about the owner of the address. The middle section (`microsoft` or `bbc`) is usually the owner's name. Collectively, the last two or three sections are known as a 'domain name'. The first section (`www`) is used to distinguish between different servers belonging to the same organisation. It's known as a 'host name'.

The rules for the last section (or sections) are confusing. They reflect the haphazard evolution of the Internet, so don't bother trying to work out the logic. The most common single-section endings are:

There are three 'global' top-level domains that are reserved for US organisations. They are .edu (education), .gov (government) and .mil (military).

.com	*com*mercial (but also used by individuals)
.org	*org*anisation (usually non-profit)
.net	Inter*net*-related businesses (such as ISPs)
.int	*int*ernational bodies (such as the United Nations)

These endings are known as 'global top-level domains', because the owner can be based anywhere in the world. Seven new ones are currently being added: .aero (air transport), .biz (businesses), .coop (co-operatives), .info (information), .museum (museums), .name (individuals) and .pro (professionals).

For a complete list of country codes, visit the web site of the Internet Assigned Numbers Authority (IANA), at (no spaces):

http://www.iana.org/cctld/cctld.htm

Two-section endings consist of an organisation code and a country code: .uk (United Kingdom), .fr (France), .de (Germany), .au (Australia), .za (South Africa) and so on. The organisation codes differ from country to country. In the UK, the most common endings are:

.co.uk	equivalent to .com
.org.uk	equivalent to .org
.net.uk	equivalent to .net
.ac.uk	academic institution (but not a school, which would have a .sch.uk address)
.gov.uk	government

Other addresses

You may also see URLs that don't begin with http://. These take you to other types of Internet site:

URL begins	Type of site
ftp://	FTP site (see page 115)
https://	Secure web site (see page 141)
mailto:	E-mail address (see page 148)
news:	Usenet newsgroup (see page 174)

Entering an address

If you know the address of the web page you wish to visit, enter it into Internet Explorer. There are three ways to do this:

If you type 'ineasysteps' (minus the quotes) and press Ctrl+Enter, 'www.' and '.com' are added for you.

1 Type the address into the Address bar, then click the Go button or press the Enter key. Internet Explorer finds and displays the page

2 Once you've visited a few sites, Internet Explorer tries to anticipate your typing. If you see the right address in the drop-down list, click on it. You don't have to press Enter

You can also click the arrow at the right-hand end of the Address bar for a list of addresses you've entered recently. This list only shows addresses you've typed yourself.

If you don't want Internet Explorer to complete your addresses, turn this feature off under Tools>Internet Options>Content>AutoComplete.

3 If you have turned off the Address bar, select Open from the File menu or press Ctrl+O. Both actions bring up the Open dialogue box. Type an address, or select one from the drop-down list. Click OK

Problems you may have

The Internet is constantly evolving: sites come and go and servers are moved or upgraded. It's also subject to its fair share of bugs and bad connections, so sometimes Internet Explorer will give you an error message instead of displaying the page you want to see:

Don't be surprised if you see something quite different. Some web sites have their own error messages with more specific information.

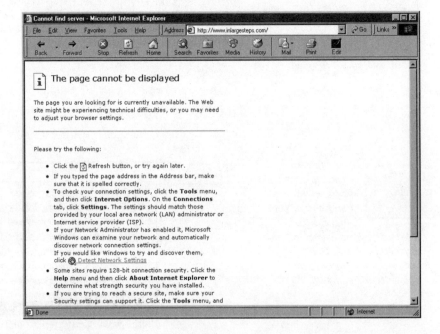

Although Internet Explorer gives you a long list of possible causes and solutions, the vast majority of errors arise because:

1   You've typed the address incorrectly. Try again, checking the address carefully before you click Go or press Enter.

2   The computer where the page is stored is temporarily out of action. Try again in a few hours' time.

3   The page you want has moved. If this is the case, Internet Explorer displays the address of the main page of the web site. Click it and try to find the page from there.

Using links

If you could only get to web pages by typing in their URLs, browsing the web would be time-consuming and tedious. Fortunately there's a much easier way to get about: links.

Almost every web page is linked to anything from one to a hundred or more other pages. Links are usually indicated by coloured, underlined text, and you move to the linked page by clicking this text. For example:

Links can also take you to another section of the same page. For example, many long pages have a list of the major subheadings at the top. Clicking on a heading takes you to the relevant subsection.

Here's a page from the Yahoo! Web directory (see page 76). If you click the blue, underlined text that says 'Arts & Humanities'…

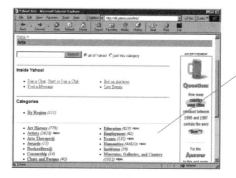

2 …you are taken to this page, which lists the Arts & Humanities subcategories. Choose a topic and click again to go to another page

You can tell when the mouse pointer is over a link, because it changes into a pointing hand ⬆. While you're pointing, check the Status bar. You should see the name of the file or site at the other end of the link. The linked text usually changes colour after you've clicked it, so you can see where you've been.

Images can also be used as links – see page 41.

Retracing your steps

Although people talk about the 'information superhighway', browsing the web is more like exploring the back streets of a market town: there are lots of directions to head in and it's easy to get lost. However, it's also easy to retrace your steps.

1   To return to the page you just left, click the Back button or press Alt+Left Arrow

You can use the History bar to return to any page you've visited in the last two or three weeks – see page 71.

2   To go back several pages, click the arrow to the right of the Back button. Select the page you want to revisit from the pop-up list

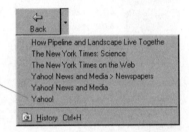

3   Once you've gone back a few pages, you may want to go forward again. Click the Forward button or press Alt+Right Arrow. If you want to go forward several pages, click the arrow to the right of the Forward button

4   If you get completely lost, you can start again by clicking the Home button or pressing Alt+Home. This takes you to your home page – the page Internet Explorer looks for each time you run it. It's usually a page from your Service Provider's web site, or a Microsoft page, but you can change it to anything you like – see page 65

Stop and Refresh

If the Internet is busy, web pages can take a long time to arrive, so Internet Explorer lets you end tedious downloads. You can then go somewhere else, or hope for a better connection and try again.

 The logo in the top right corner is animated when a page is downloading and becomes static when the transfer is complete. You can click on links as soon as you see the text, though – you don't have to wait for the rest of the page to arrive.

1 To abort a download, click the Stop button, select View>Stop or press Esc. Internet Explorer gives up fetching the page

2 If you change your mind and want to see the rest of a half-downloaded page, click the Refresh button, select View>Refresh or press F5 to reload the page. You should also click Refresh if you think Internet Explorer isn't displaying a page correctly

3 You can use Refresh to make sure you're seeing the very latest version of a page. For example, pages showing sports results may be updated every few minutes, but the new data won't necessarily be sent to your computer. Sites that work this way usually tell you to 'reload often'

Understanding web pages

Web pages start out as unformatted text files – the type of file your word processor produces when you save a document as 'text' or 'plain text'. The designer then specifies how the page should look by inserting pairs of 'tags'. To emphasise a phrase by displaying it in bold type, for example, they insert a 'bold on' tag at the beginning and a 'bold off' tag at the end. When you download the file, Internet Explorer reads the tags and adds the formatting.

To see what an HTML file really looks like, open a web page and select View>Source. Internet Explorer transfers the file to Notepad, which displays the tags (look for things in angle <> brackets) as well as the text.

This system is known as HyperText Mark-up Language (HTML). As well as enabling web designers to format their pages, it makes it possible to include references to other files. For example, links are created using a pair of tags that say, 'If someone clicks anywhere between here (link on) and here (link off), load file xyz.' It might not sound very exciting, but without the ability to include these instructions in the pages, the whole thing would fall apart. You'd have to know the location of every single page instead of just jumping from one to the next.

Additional uses for tags

Tags can also be used to tell the browser to download additional files and insert them into the text. This is how the images arrive: Internet Explorer reads the HTML file, finds an instruction that tells it to 'insert image abc', fetches the image file, works out how everything should look and displays the page. This is why the text often appears first: until you download the HTML file, Internet Explorer doesn't even know there should be pictures.

Unless you want to create your own web pages, you don't need to worry about the ins and outs of HTML. However, it's worth remembering that the pictures are stored separately from the text, as are sounds, animations and video clips.

Images

Before the web was invented, the Internet was a text-based medium. You could access lots of useful information from around the globe and many interesting discussions were held. However, it all looked about as exciting as pages from the phone book, so no-one wanted to put the Internet on television. It was clever, but it wasn't pretty.

If you see an icon with a red cross [x] *where an image should be, Internet Explorer either can't find or can't display the image file.*

The addition of images changed all that. They make the web colourful and interesting, add personality and give it a friendly face. They're used to illustrate news stories and travel guides, to liven up personal web pages, to show you products in on-line shops, and to create fancy buttons and headings. The web wouldn't be the same without them.

Images can be displayed as part of a web page, or on their own. In the first case, Internet Explorer slots the picture(s) into the text, according to the web designer's instructions. In the second, it simply displays the picture in the main window. To find out whether you're looking at a whole page or just a single image, look at the Address bar. If the address ends in .gif, .jpg, .jpeg or .png, you're viewing an image.

To turn an image into Windows wallpaper, right-click on it, then select Set as Background from the pop-up menu.

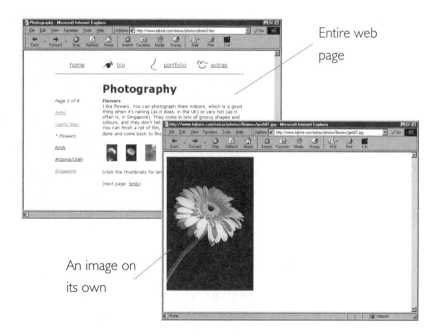

Entire web page

An image on its own

Image toolbar

If you hold the mouse pointer over an image, without clicking, a small toolbar may appear. It has four buttons that enable you to do things with the image.

1 Save the image

2 Print the image

3 Attach the image to an e-mail message so you can send it to a friend (see Chapter 8)

4 Open the My Pictures folder. You can copy the image into this folder by dragging it across with the mouse

When you view an image on its own, rather than as part of a web page, a second control may appear in the bottom right corner. This means Internet Explorer has resized the image to make it fit into the main window.

1 Click to expand the image to its normal size. Use the scroll bars to move around

2 Click again to make the image fit in the window

Images as links

Images aren't just used to make the pages pretty; they can also help you get from one to the next. The four most common types of image link are:

1   *Buttons* – many web sites use icons and toolbars to help you navigate. For example, the Yahoo! Web directory (see page 76) has buttons that take you to special sections of the site.

2   *Text* – when web designers want to use a special font, create fancy text effects or combine text with graphics, they have to save the text in an image file. The result doesn't look like regular linked text, but it functions the same way. For example, the Yahoo! logo appears in the top left corner of all the site's pages. If you click it, you're taken back to the main page.

3   *Image maps* – some images contain more than one link. For example, the BBC web site (see page 85) included this map of the All England Club in its coverage of Wimbledon 2001. When you clicked on one of the black areas, you got more information about the selected court or building.

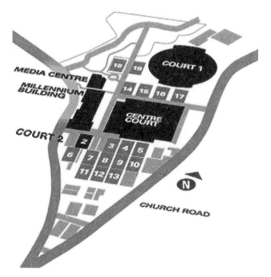

4 *Thumbnails* – because large images take a long time to download, web designers often show you small preview versions first. For example, if you visit the Internet Movie Database (see page 84) and look at one of the photo galleries, you'll get a page like this. Click the thumbnail images to see larger versions of the photographs.

Photo gallery for Pearl Harbor

Studio Stills Images

Click on a photo below to see it in a larger size.

Still photographs of "Pearl Harbor"

You can find out whether an image is a link by moving the mouse pointer over it. If it changes to a pointing hand, just as it does over a text link (see page 35), clicking will take you to another page.

Sounds and videos

Some web sites have background music that plays automatically when you download a page. If a tune is getting on your nerves, click Stop to halt the playback.

It's more common for audio and video files to be linked to the page, so you can decide whether you want to play them.

To save a sound or video clip onto your hard disk, right-click the link that leads to it and select Save Target As. This doesn't always work – some files can't be saved.

1 To play a sound or video clip, such as these shuttle videos from the Human Spaceflight section of NASA's web site (see page 100), click the link that leads to the file. You may need to select the speed of your connection

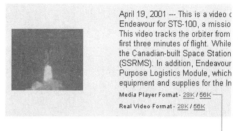

April 19, 2001 --- This is a video of Endeavour for STS-100, a missio This video tracks the orbiter from first three minutes of flight. While the Canadian-built Space Station (SSRMS). In addition, Endeavour Purpose Logistics Module, which equipment and supplies for the In

Media Player Format · 28K / 56K
Real Video Format · 28K / 56K

2 If Internet Explorer can play the clip, it offers to do so. Click the Yes button to proceed

Playback begins quickly because this video clip is stored in a streaming format – see page 45.

3 Internet Explorer displays the Media bar on the left of the main window and downloads the clip. It starts playing automatically

4 Use the Play/Pause and Stop buttons to control the playback

5 Use the Volume slider to adjust the volume

6   If you'd rather play the clip in a separate window, click the Undock Player button:

7   Playback continues in the new window. To transfer the video clip back to the Media bar, click the Redock Player button

If Internet Explorer can play a sound or video file, it does. If it can't, it may automatically transfer the file to another program – see Chapter 6. Sometimes it can't do that either, usually because you haven't got the required software. If you're having problems playing sounds or videos from a particular web site, see if there's an information page that tells you what software you need and where to get it from.

Streaming sound and video

Some sound and video files have to be downloaded before you can play them back. This can take a long time. For example, a four-minute song saved in the MP3 format might take 16 minutes to download. If it were saved in the Windows Audio (.wav) format, you'd have to wait even longer.

Some web sites provide several versions of each sound file or video, optimised for streaming at different speeds. Pick the one that matches the speed of your connection.

Streaming sound and video formats were invented to speed things up. They are compressed so each minute of sound or video takes a minute to download. This means you can play the 'stream' as it downloads, rather than afterwards.

Streaming formats can't compete with traditional sound and video files for audio and picture quality, because a lot of data has to be stripped out to keep downloading and playback in sync. However, you get to see or hear something seconds after you click on a link.

Streaming is used to transmit radio and television shows over the Internet, and for live 'webcasts' of special events. It can also be used for prerecorded material. For example, CD merchants such as CD Universe (see page 93) often let you listen to sample tracks so you can make sure you're buying the right disk.

Common streaming formats include RealAudio, RealVideo, QuickTime, Windows Media Audio and Windows Media Video.

Internet Explorer can play Windows Media files, but you'll need additional software for the others – see Chapter 6.

You need the latest version of Windows Media Player to get the best out of Windows Media files. Download it from (no spaces):

http://www.microsoft.com/ windows/windowsmedia/ en/default.asp

Downloading program files

You can download lots of software from the Internet, including public domain and shareware programs, demo versions of commercial software and add-ons for many programs. Internet Explorer enables you to fetch and run these files in a single operation, but you'll almost always want to save them on to your hard disk instead. You can experiment with your new software once you've disconnected from the Internet.

I To download a program file, e.g. this screensaver from *The New York Times* (see page 82), click the appropriate link

Screensavers

Get a FREE NYTimes.com photo screensaver and enjoy these popular photographs every day on your desktop computer.

There's always a chance that a downloaded program might contain a virus. See page 135 for advice.

2 Internet Explorer asks whether you want to open (run) the file or save it on to your hard disk. Click the Save button

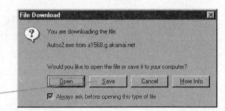

3 The standard Save As dialogue box appears. Select a folder and click the Save button

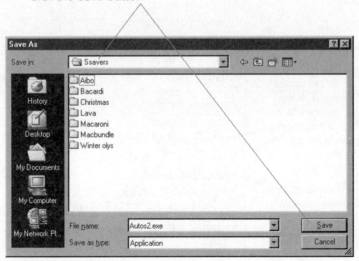

4 The file is downloaded onto your hard disk – this often takes several minutes. You can continue browsing or switch to another application and carry on working

5 Once the download is complete, you have three options. Click Open to run the program straightaway

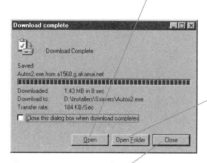

6 Or, click Open Folder to find the file on your hard disk

7 Or, click Close to close the dialogue box and go on with something else. Don't forget to go back and deal with your new program later!

Compressed files

Web designers often use compression programs to 'archive' the program files linked to their pages. Creating an archive packs everything – setup utility, documentation, help files and the program itself – into a single, neat package. The archive is substantially smaller than the original group of files, so it downloads more quickly.

You'll also come across self-extracting archives. These have an .exe extension and unzip themselves automatically when you run them.

The most popular compression program on the PC, PKZIP, produces archives with a .zip extension. Follow the instructions on the previous page to save them on to your hard disk.

Once you have downloaded a .zip file, you'll need to decompress or 'unzip' it. There are numerous shareware unzippers – try PKZIP for Windows or WinZip.

You can get PKZIP from PKWARE's web site at:
`http://www.pkware.com/`

WinZip is available from Niko Mak Computing at:
`http://www.winzip.com/`

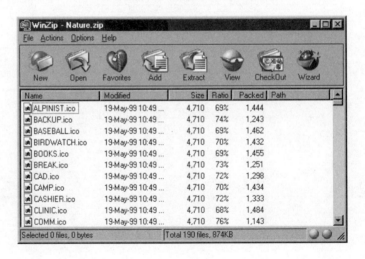

Other types of archive you may encounter include .hqx, .sit, .sea (Macintosh), .gz, .Z, .tar and .gtar (Unix) files. It's unlikely you'll be able to use the contents of these files, so it's best to avoid them.

Saving web pages

Sometimes you'll come across a web page with information you might want to refer to in the future. Saving it on to your hard disk enables you to reload it whenever you want, without the expense of logging on and downloading it again.

See page 85 for more about the BBC web site.

1 To save a web page, pull down the File menu and select Save As. This brings up the Save As dialogue box

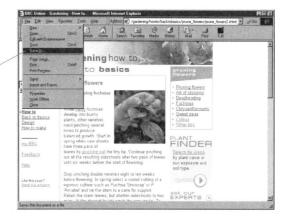

2 Choose a folder and give the file a name

Don't forget that material on the web is protected by copyright. Keeping copies for personal reference is unlikely to get you into trouble, but you mustn't reuse or redistribute text, images, sounds or videos without permission.

3 Select 'Web Page, complete' to save the text and the pictures as separate files

4 Or, select 'Web Archive, single file' to store everything in one file

5 Or, select 'Web Page, HTML only' to save the text and the formatting instructions

6 Or, select 'Text File' to just save the text, without formatting

7 Click Save

8 'Web Page, complete' produces an .htm file for the page and a folder full of picture files

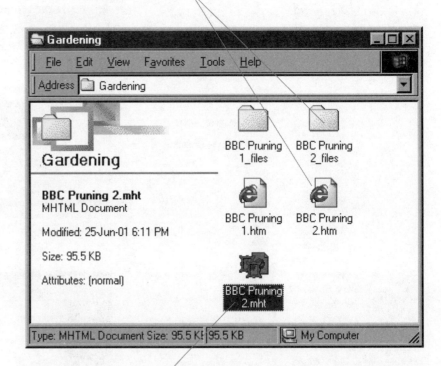

9 'Web Archive, single file' produces a file with an .mht extension

10 Either way, you can load the page back into Internet Explorer by double-clicking on the file. Alternatively, select Open from Internet Explorer's File menu. Click the Browse button to find the file

Printing web pages

If you're gathering information for a report or project, printing web pages is sometimes more convenient than saving them. You don't end up with a hard disk full of web pages and you can scribble notes in the margins or highlight important passages. You can also print a table showing all the web pages linked to the current one.

1 To print the current page, pull down the File menu and select Print. Alternatively, press Ctrl+P

If you're only interested in a couple of paragraphs of text, highlight them with the mouse before you go to File> Print. In Step 2, choose 'Selection'.

2 Decide whether to print the whole document or specified pages (see overleaf)

3 If the page has frames (see page 110), you need to tell Internet Explorer how they should be handled

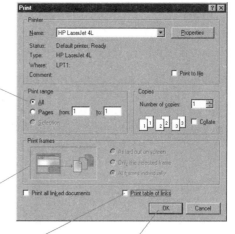

You can also print a page by clicking the Print button on the toolbar, but you'll bypass the Print dialogue and won't be able to change any of the options.

4 To include details of any linked web pages, select 'Print table of links'

5 Click the OK button to print the page

Print Preview

Because web pages are designed to be viewed on a monitor, they don't always print the way you expect them to. If you use Internet Explorer's Print Preview function, you get more control over the output. Sometimes it's enough to make the difference between wasting paper and producing a useful printout.

1 To preview your printout, select File>Print Preview

To decode the header and footer codes in the Setup box, click the Help button ? *in the top right corner, then click on the Header or Footer settings.*

2 To change the margins, header, footer and/or page orientation, click the Setup button:

3 Use these controls to move from page to page

4 Use these controls to zoom in or out

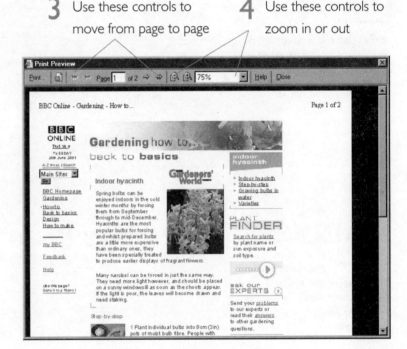

5 Once you're happy, click the Print button.

Print Preview lets you see which pages contain useful information. When you click Print, you can use the 'Print range' options (Step 2, previous page) to omit the others.

Getting help

Internet Explorer has a web-style Help file that's handy if you need to check something while you're on-line.

1 To open the Help file, go to Help > Contents and Index

2 Click a chapter title, then select a topic. The text is displayed on the right

3 Some pages have links to related material

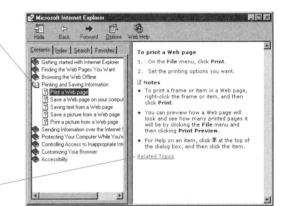

4 If you can't find the topic you want, click the Index tab

5 Type in a keyword

6 The relevant section of the index appears. Double-click a topic to display it on the right

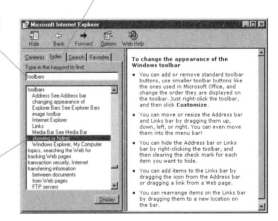

...cont'd

You can access the Support section of Microsoft's web site by selecting Help>Online Support. However, the information you'll find there is aimed at expert users.

7 Still need more information? Click the Search tab

8 Enter your keyword again

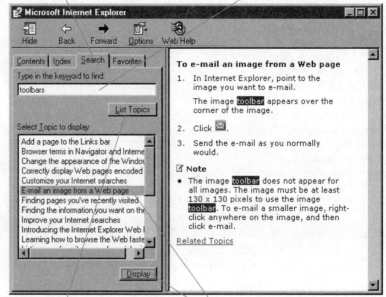

9 Click the List Topics button

10 This time you see all the topics that mention your keyword. Select a topic and click Display to read about it in the right-hand pane

Finding your way

There are over a billion web pages and it's easy to lose your way as you jump from one to the next. This chapter explains how to use Favorites, Shortcuts and the Links bar to keep track of the ones you visit regularly. It also shows you how to find information on the web.

Covers

Chapter Three

Creating Favorites

As you explore the web, you'll often come across sites you'll want to visit again in the future. Rather than writing down the address, add the site to Internet Explorer's Favorites menu.

You can also right-click on the page and select Add to Favorites from the pop-up menu. Right-click on a link to create a Favorite for the web page at the other end.

1 To create a Favorite for the current page, select Add to Favorites from the Favorites menu

The 'Make available offline' option is covered on page 61.

2 Check the name – you may need to change it to something shorter or clearer. Click OK to create the Favorite

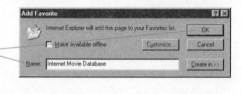

See page 84 to find out more about the Internet Movie Database.

3 You can return to this page whenever you want, simply by selecting it from the Favorites menu

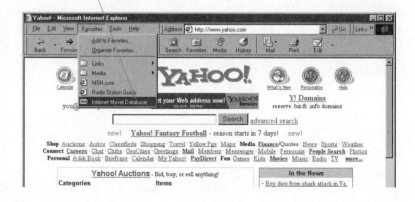

Managing Favorites

Once you have 15–20 Favorites, you'll need to start organising them into folders. This creates submenus and makes it easier to find the one you want.

You'll already have a Links folder (see page 64) and a Media folder.

1 Select Organize Favorites in the Favorites menu

2 Click the Create Folder button

3 Type in a name and press Enter

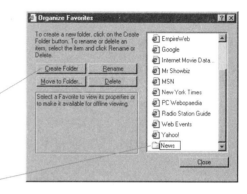

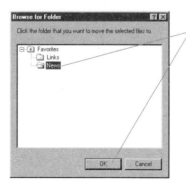

4 Select a Favorite that needs to be relocated into the new folder. Internet Explorer displays its details on the left

5 Click Move to Folder

You can also drag Favorites to the correct folders.

6 Select the folder and click OK

7 Click Close to finish organising your Favorites

To save a new Favorite straight into a folder, click the Create in>> button (see Step 2 on page 56). Select the folder, then click OK.

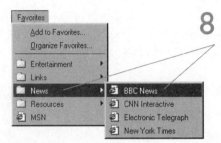

8 Your Favorites menu now has submenus. To access them, hold the mouse pointer over the folder's menu entry until the submenu appears

Managing Favorites with Windows Explorer

All your Favorites are stored on your hard disk, each in its own file, in the C:\Windows\Favorites folder. You can view them using Windows Explorer. Once you have a lot of Favorites, you may find it easier to organise them using this program, which lets you drag them around in groups.

Want to back up all your Favorites? Return to Internet Explorer and select File> Import and Export. The Import/Export Wizard will help you export all your Favorites into a single file. Copy this file on to a floppy disk for safekeeping.

1 Run Windows Explorer and locate the Favorites folder

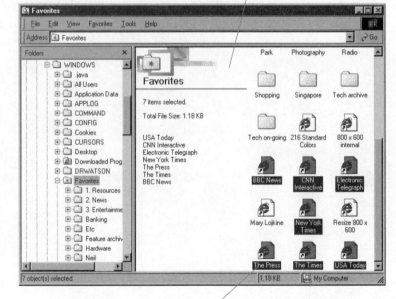

2 Use File>New> Folder to create any new folders

3 Select your Favorites, holding down Shift or Ctrl to select several at once, and drag them to the correct folder

Favorites bar

The Favorites bar gives you another way to access your Favorites. It's more convenient than the menu, but takes up quite a lot of the main window.

1 Click the Favorites button to open the Favorites bar

2 Click a folder to see a list of Favorites. A second click closes the folder

3 Click a Favorite to open a web page (in this case, the BBC's News site – see page 81)

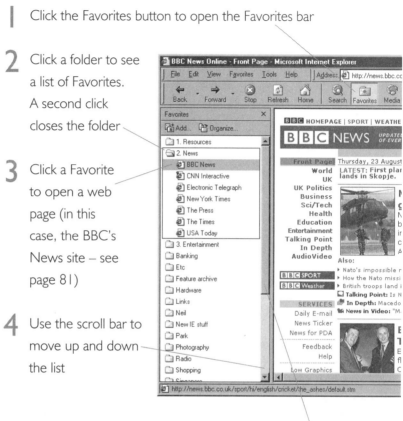

4 Use the scroll bar to move up and down the list

5 Drag the divider left or right to change the size of the bar

6 Click the Favorites button again to close the Favorites bar. You can also click the cross ⌧ in the top right corner

Managing Favorites with the Favorites bar

You can use the Favorites bar to reorganise your Favorites. It enables you to move, delete and rename both Favorites and folders. You can also change their order.

1 Click Add to create a Favorite for the page you're currently viewing (see page 56)

2 Click Organize to open the Organize Favorites dialogue box (see page 57)

3 To delete a folder or Favorite, right-click on it and select Delete from the pop-up menu

4 To change the Favorite's name, select Rename instead

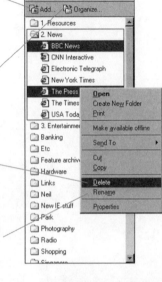

You can use all these tricks in the Favorites menu, too. There's even an extra option: when you right-click on a folder or Favorite, you can choose Sort by Name to sort that section of the menu into alphabetical order.

5 To move a folder or Favorite, point to it with the mouse, then press and hold the left button

6 Drag the selected item to a new location. You can move it to a particular position in the list by looking out for the black divider that appears when the mouse pointer is between two items

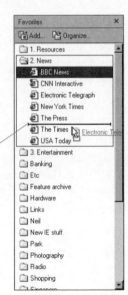

Browsing pages off-line

If you have a laptop, you may want to download pages from your favourite news site while you eat breakfast, then read them on the train. Internet Explorer can copy material from selected web pages into a folder on your hard disk, enabling you to access the information without reconnecting to the Internet.

1 To mark the pages that you want to download, go to Favorites> Organize Favorites

2 Select the web site you're interested in, then select the Make available offline checkbox

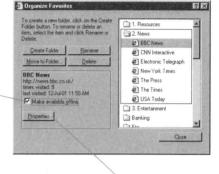

3 The front page of a news site often gives you the headlines, then provides links to the stories. To fetch linked pages, click Properties

4 Click the Download tab

HOT TIP
Don't go more than one link deep unless the site has very few links.

5 Set 'Download pages...' to one link deep

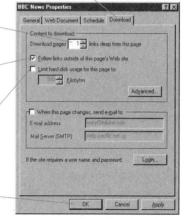

6 Decide whether you want to follow links to other servers

7 If you're short of disk space, you may want to set a limit for this site

HOT TIP
If in doubt, follow external links and don't set a limit for the site. You can come back and change these options later if there's a problem.

8 Click OK

9 Repeat steps 2–8 for any other sites you want to download

Selecting the 'Make available offline' checkbox marks a site for download. However, the files aren't actually fetched until you tell Internet Explorer to synchronise the pages on your hard disk with the ones on the Internet (it may do this spontaneously when you first select a site).

Synchronising

When you synchronise your computer, Internet Explorer checks whether the pages you've selected have been updated and downloads any new material.

The pages you download are stored in the Temporary Internet Files folder, otherwise known as the 'cache'. You may need to allocate extra space to this folder if you want to view a lot of pages off-line.

To do this, go to Tools> Internet Options and click the General tab. In the Temporary Internet Files section, click Settings. Move the slider to increase the capacity of this folder.

1 Go to the Tools menu and select Synchronize

2 Click the checkboxes of the sites you want to download

3 Click Synchronize

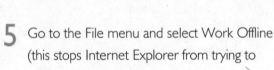

4 Internet Explorer checks for updates and downloads any pages that have changed. When it has finished, log off

5 Go to the File menu and select Work Offline (this stops Internet Explorer from trying to connect to the Internet)

6 Use the Favorites menu or Favorites bar to call up the pages you've downloaded. They'll have red stars on their icons

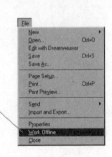

Internet shortcuts

An Internet shortcut is a Favorite that lives on your Windows Desktop, rather than in the Favorites menu. Double-clicking on it runs Internet Explorer, connects you to the Internet and takes you to the specified page.

Internet shortcuts are useful for sites you visit frequently. For example, you could use a shortcut to the BBC's News site (see page 81) to start Internet Explorer first thing in the morning. Later in the day you might want to use a search engine or go straight to a sports or entertainment site.

If you can see some of your Desktop alongside Internet Explorer's window, you can also make shortcuts using the page icon at the left-hand end of the Address bar:

Drag it on to your desktop to make a Shortcut for the current page.

1   To create an Internet shortcut, right-click on the background of the web page and select Create Shortcut from the pop-up menu. Alternatively, go to File>Send>Shortcut To Desktop

2   A dialogue box appears. Click OK to confirm the creation of the shortcut

3   The shortcut is placed on your desktop.

4   To give it a better name, click on it once, wait a couple of seconds and then click again. Type in a short, descriptive name

5   Double-click the shortcut to start Internet Explorer and load the specified page (if Internet Explorer is already running, clicking the shortcut just takes you to the page)

Links bar

The Links bar provides another way to access your favourite sites. When you install Internet Explorer, it contains buttons for sites selected by Microsoft or your Service Provider. You can replace these with your own top choices.

1. If you don't find the default links useful, right-click on them and select Delete from the pop-up menu

You can also make a button for the current page by dragging the page icon:

from the Address bar to the Links bar.

2. There are several ways to create new buttons. To add the page you're currently viewing, select Add to Favorites from the Favorites menu. Click the Create in>> button and select the Links folder

3. Another option is to open the Favourites bar and drag a few of your Favorites on to the Links bar. You need to place them alongside the existing buttons – a black divider appears when the mouse is in the right place

Why do some sites have fancy icons? This is up to the web designer – if they create a special icon, Internet Explorer uses it. To change an icon, right-click on it and select Properties. Click the Change Icon button and choose another design.

4. You can also select a link on a web page and add the page at the other end to the Links bar. Point to the link, hold down the right mouse button and drag it on to the bar

5. If you add more sites than Internet Explorer can display, an arrow button appears at the right-hand end of the bar. Click it to see the rest of the buttons in a list

Home Page

The term 'Home Page' has several meanings. It can also refer to a personal web page or the main page of a web site.

Internet Explorer looks for the Home Page each time you run it. You're also taken to this page when you click the Home button or press Alt+Home.

The default Home Page is usually one of your Service Provider's web pages, although you may be taken to Microsoft's web page instead. You don't have to stick with the default setting, though – you can change the Home Page to any page you visit often or find useful, such as a news site or web directory.

If you know the URL, you can type it into the Address box.

1 To change your Home Page, browse to the site you'd like to use. Select Tools>Internet Options and click the General tab

2 Click Use Current to change your Home Page

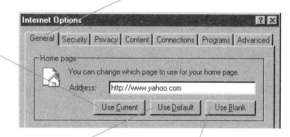

3 Or, click Use Default to revert to the Home Page that was specified when you installed Internet Explorer

4 Or, click Use Blank if you often want to run Internet Explorer without connecting to the Internet. It will load a blank page from your hard disk instead of running the connection software

Searching the Internet

Browsing aimlessly around the Internet is easy – you keep clicking links until you come across something interesting. More often than not, though, you'll be looking for specific information. If you were in a library, you'd consult the catalogue; on the Internet, you turn to the organisations and individuals who devote their time to indexing the World Wide Web.

There are three basic types of index. Directories list sites by topic and subtopic, enabling you to focus in on the area of interest gradually. If you are looking for an explanation of Albert Einstein's Theory of Relativity, for example, you select Science, and then Physics, Relativity and so on. Web directories work well when you're researching a broad area.

In addition to search engines that cover the entire web, you'll come across more specialised ones that concentrate on particular topics or sites. The technology is the same; they just use a smaller database.

If you're looking for something more specific, you're better off using a search engine. Search engines enable you to search or 'query' a vast database that indexes all the text on millions of web pages. You type in a few keywords – 'Albert', 'Einstein' and 'relativity', perhaps – and the site returns a list of all the web pages where they appear. In most cases you get a brief extract that helps you work out which pages are relevant.

Search engines are thorough but not very bright. They'll often return thousands or tens of thousands of 'hits', all of which contain your keywords, but few of which answer your question. If you choose your keywords carefully, though (see page 70), they can be very efficient.

The third type of index is a meta-list – a page of links dedicated to a particular subject, sometimes with brief descriptions of each site. Meta-lists are usually prepared by people who've spent a lot of time tracking down useful sites and want to share the results.

A search may take you through all three types of index. A web directory might point you to a meta-list, which might recommend a site, which in turn might have a search engine that helps you find the most relevant page.

Search Assistant

Internet Explorer's Search Assistant provides easy access to several search engines. It displays the Search controls down the left-hand side of the screen, enabling you to keep the results in view while you check out individual sites.

1 Click the Search button to open the Search Assistant

2 Tell the Search Assistant what you're trying to find

3 Enter your keywords

You can conduct a quick search from the Address bar.
Type 'go', 'find' or '?' followed by the word(s) you want to find, then press Enter.

4 Click Search

5 A list of pages appears on the left

6 When you click a link, the corresponding web page is displayed on the right

When you find a good site, go to Tools>Show Related Links to open another bar that lists sites that have something in common with the current one.

7 To send the keywords to another search engine, click Next. Click the arrow alongside the Next button to select a specific engine

The controls you see when you click the Search button aren't loaded from your hard disk; you're actually looking at a page from Microsoft's web site. Microsoft sometimes changes this page to add new search engines. Don't be surprised if you open the Search Assistant and find extra choices.

8 Click New when you're ready to start another search

9 The 'Previous searches' option lets you reuse old keywords

10 The 'Find a map' option locates places or landmarks

11 You can also search for files or folders on your computer; computers on your network; or people's e-mail addresses

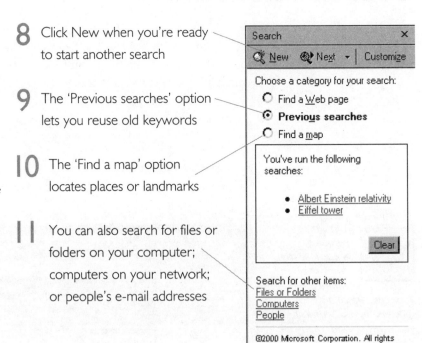

The Search Assistant is convenient, but its range of search engines is quite limited, and it doesn't tell you how to make the most of them. It's a good idea to visit their Home Pages (see pages 76–78 for some addresses) to find out about any special facilities they offer.

Customising the Search Assistant

You'll probably find that some search engines are more helpful than others, and you may not use some of the Search Assistant's categories. Clear out the dead wood by using the Customize option to fine-tune your choices.

1 Open the Search Assistant and click the Customize button

If you don't like the Search Assistant and just want to use your favourite search engine, select 'Use one search service for all searches'.

2 Select the categories and search engines you want to use

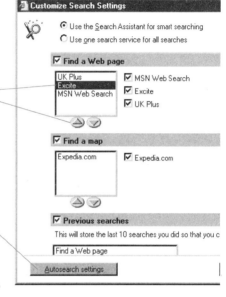

3 Move your favourite engine to the top of the list, so it is used first. To do this, select it and click the blue 'up' button

4 Click Autosearch settings to decide which engine is used for Address bar searches (see the HOT TIP on page 67)

5 Click OK to finish, or Reset to go back to the default settings, or Cancel to go back to Internet Explorer without implementing your changes

6 You may need to close and restart Internet Explorer to see the effect of your changes

Searching tips

Searching the Internet can be frustrating, but with practice it's possible to locate information quickly and efficiently.

Bear the following pointers in mind:

1   Decide whether you're searching or browsing. If you're looking for general information about a broad topic, such as 'relativity', use a directory to find sites that concentrate on that subject. If you're looking for a specific person or event, use a search engine.

2   Visit the search engine's Home Page, find the instructions and read them. The popular services all have different options, and what works with one won't necessarily work with another. Once you've found an engine you like, stick with it – the others may find a slightly different selection of sites, but you won't miss much.

If you're taken to a long page and can't work out where your keywords appear, select Edit>Find or press Ctrl+F to search the text.

3   Think words, not concepts. Most search engines look for documents containing your keywords, so don't try to describe the concept – you'll get better results by thinking of terms that are likely to appear in the text of a relevant web page.

4   Refine your search with phrases and extra terms. Most engines allow you to specify that two or more words should appear together, or that the documents must contain some words and not others. For example, searching for 'Einstein' finds over 300,000 pages. Searching for the phrase 'Albert Einstein' brings the total down to 23,000.

5   Use alternatives. Try 'movie' as well as 'film', and don't forget that 'football' is 'soccer' in many parts of the world.

History bar

If there's any chance you might want to return to a page, it's a good idea to make a Favorite or Shortcut for it. However, all isn't lost if you haven't. You can use the History bar to return to any page you've visited in the last couple of weeks.

See page 85 to find out more about the BBC web site.

Use the mouse to point to one of the listed pages, without clicking. You'll get a pop-up label showing the full name and address.

1 Click the History button to open the History bar

2 Click the correct day, then find the server where the page resides

3 When you find the page you want to return to, click the title to load it into the main window

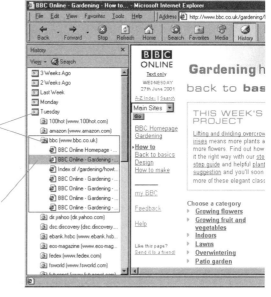

4 If you can't find the page you want to see, click the View button to sort the bar another way

5 Select By Site if you know where a page was, but can't remember when you last visited it

6 Or, use By Most Visited to bring your favourite sites to the top of the list

7 Or, use By Order Visited Today to review today's browsing

Searching your History

You can hunt through your History for sites that cover a particular subject.

1 Click Search

2 Enter your keyword

3 Click Search Now

4 Relevant pages are listed down the left. Click one to display it on the right

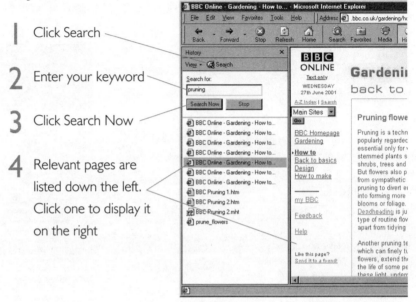

Changing the storage period

You can specify how long the records should be kept. You might want to increase the storage period if you don't log on very often.

1 Go to Options. Click the General tab

2 Use the up/down arrows to adjust the number of days information remains in the History folder

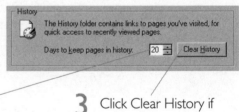

3 Click Clear History if you want to delete your records and start afresh

4 Click OK to finish

Exploring the web

The Internet has so much to offer that it's hard to know where to start. The best way to learn about the web is by exploring it, so here's a selection of useful, interesting and entertaining sites that provide a good introduction.

Covers

Chapter Four

Microsoft

Microsoft

`http://www.microsoft.com/`

Microsoft's web site has lots of information about the company's products, including Windows, Word, Excel, Encarta and, of course, Internet Explorer. You can download demos and add-ons, learn about new technologies or use the Support section to solve technical problems. The Knowledge Base – a database of solutions and step-by-step guides used by Microsoft's technical-support people – is worth a look if one of your applications is playing up.

A 'mirror' is a copy of a web site on another server, often in a different part of the world.

There's also a European mirror of Microsoft's site. It isn't as busy as the main site, so pages and files download quickly. Find it at:
`http://www.eu.microsoft.com/`

There's a UK-specific site at:
`http://www.microsoft.com/uk/`

The Internet

CNET

http://www.cnet.com/

CNET is a vast American web site covering computers, the Internet and consumer electronics. It offers a mixture of news, reviews and features, plus software to download. Sometimes it seems too big for its own good, but if you click around you'll discover plenty of beginner-friendly items, including 'how to' guides and backgrounders that help you make sense of new technologies.

You could also try:

WiredNews, an electronic spin-off of US Internet magazine *Wired*, for another dose of news and culture. Find it at:
http://www.wired.com/

For a UK perspective, try the on-line versions of computer magazines *.net* and *Internet Magazine*:
http://www.netmag.co.uk/
http://www.internet-magazine.com/

Directories

Yahoo!

`http://www.yahoo.com/`

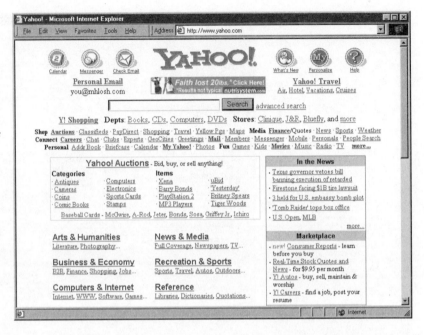

Yahoo! is a hierarchical directory of web sites and (some) other Internet resources. Each of the 14 categories is progressively subdivided into more tightly defined subcategories, enabling you to work your way down to a list of sites that concentrate on the subject of interest.

Yahoo! has several more specialised offshoots, including Yahooligans! for younger browsers, Yahoo! UK & Ireland and the customisable My Yahoo!

You could also try:

About, which employs human guides to catalogue the best sites on over 700 subjects. Find it at:

`http://www.about.com/`

UK Plus, a family-friendly web directory 'dedicated to finding and reviewing everything that a UK reader might consider worth seeing on the Internet'. Find it at:

`http://www.ukplus.co.uk/`

Search engines

AltaVista

http://www.altavista.com/

Search engines and directories are some of the most popular sites on the web. Many offer additional services and the line between directories and search engines has become very indistinct.

AltaVista enables you to search for web sites containing a particular word or phrase. Click the Help link to read the instructions – you'll get results more quickly once you know how to phrase your query. You can also hunt for images, video clips, audio clips and news stories. If you end up at a web page in Spanish, French, German, Italian, Portuguese, Japanese, Korean or Chinese, use the Babel Fish utility to translate it into English.

You could also try:

AltaVista UK, which lets you concentrate on UK sites, at:
http://www.altavista.co.uk/

Google, a powerful engine with a simple interface, at:
http://www.google.com/

Ask Jeeves, which accepts plain-English questions, at:
http://www.askjeeves.com/

Specialised search engines

Yahoo! People Search

`http://people.yahoo.com/`

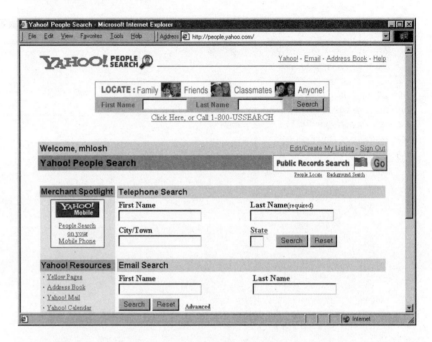

Forgotten someone's e-mail address? Type their name into Yahoo!'s People Search and it may turn up their details. If you want to make it easier for people to contact you, add your own listing to the directory.

You could also try:

Google Groups, which indexes messages posted to Usenet newsgroups (see Chapter 9), at:
`http://groups.google.com/`

File2k, to find sites on FTP sites (see page 115), at:
`http://www.file2k.com/`

CNET's Search.com enables you to access over 800 specialist search engines. Find it at:
`http://www.search.com/`

Best and worst

The web 100
http://www.web100.com/

The Web 100 lists the best sites on the web, as voted for by Internet users. The list is updated every hour, can be viewed by subject as well as ranking, and includes a brief review of each site. Some are too US-oriented to hold much interest for British Internet users, but there are plenty of big-name sites with international appeal.

You could also try:
Netsurfer Digest, a weekly newsletter covering interesting sites. Sign up to receive it by e-mail at:
http://www.netsurf.com/nsd/

Project Cool, for sites that are innovative or beautifully designed. The Sightings section provides a daily link.
http://www.projectcool.com/

The Useless Pages, for a selection of completely pointless (but entertaining) web sites, at:
http://www.go2net.com/internet/useless/

Service Providers

Internet Magazine

`http://www.internet-magazine.com/isp/`

Internet Magazine maintains a database of Internet Service Providers, with details of their offerings and links to their web sites. You can find a service by name or search for services with particular features.

You could also try:

Easy as 1-2-Free catalogues Service Providers that don't charge a monthly subscription. Find it at:
`http://www.12free.co.uk/`

The Cybercafe Search Engine lists cyber cafés and public Internet access points in over 150 countries. Find it at:
`http://www.cybercaptive.com/`

Don't forget to visit your Service Provider's web site, which may provide technical support as well as details of its services. The information you were sent when you opened your account should include the site's address.

News

The Electronic Telegraph
http://www.telegraph.co.uk/

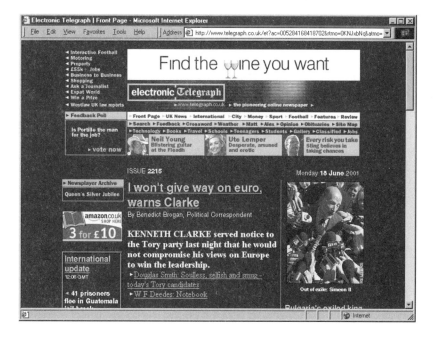

The on-line edition of *The Telegraph* has everything you'd expect in a printed newspaper, including UK, international and City news, sport, weather, a crossword, cartoons and classified ads. Catch up on older stories by searching the archive, which goes back to November 1994.

You could also try:

BBC News, a typically polished effort with all the headlines plus audio and video, background articles and 'Talking Point' areas where you can vote on topical issues. Find it at:
http://news.bbc.co.uk/

Ananova, a virtual newscaster with green hair. She reads out the headlines on demand at:
http://www.ananova.com/

NewsNow, for links to the top stories from over 100 other news services, sorted by country and category. Find it at:
http://www.newsnow.co.uk/

CNN Interactive

http://www.cnn.com/

One of the great things about the Internet is the tremendous choice of viewpoints. As well as browsing British news sites, you can pop over to the United States for an American perspective on US and world news.

CNN's site provides a wide range of clearly presented stories, complete with sound samples and video clips. It's updated throughout the day and there are lots of cross-references and links to other sites.

You could also try:

The New York Times, for in-depth coverage of international and US news. Find it at:

http://www.nyt.com/

Kidon Media-Link, for links to on-line news services from all around the globe, at:

http://www.kidon.com/media-link/

Weather

The BBC Weather Centre

http://www.bbc.co.uk/weather/

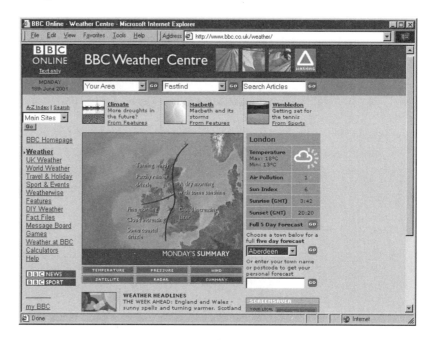

Come rain or shine, the BBC Weather Centre brings you forecasts, weather lore and information about its services. You can meet the team and find out how they produce around 100 forecasts every weekday, or see how this year's weather is measuring up. Other features include a glossary, a temperature convertor, instructions for setting up your own weather station and weather-related games.

You could also try:

The Met Office, for national, regional and marine forecasts and information about weather forecasting, at:

http://www.meto.gov.uk/

Weather.com, the web site of The Weather Channel, for forecasts for cities all around the world. Find it at:

http://www.weather.com/

Entertainment: Movies

The Internet Movie Database
`http://uk.imdb.com/`

The Internet Movie Database contains everything you're likely to want to know about over 250,000 movies. As well as cast lists, synopses, reviews, trailers, photos and trivia, it has links to official studio sites and fan pages for directors and actors.

You could also try:

Mr Showbiz, an entertaining celebrity-oriented site that supplements its news and reviews with profiles, interviews, and polls. Find it at:
`http://mrshowbiz.go.com/`

Most major releases have promotional web sites with pictures, sound and video clips, games and so on. Use the Internet Movie Database to track them down.

Television

BBC Online
http://www.bbc.co.uk/

BBC Online is the BBC's public-service offering. In addition to news (see page 81) and weather (see page 83), it has information about everything from *TeleTubbies* and *Blue Peter* to *EastEnders*, *Tomorrow's World* and *WatchDog*. You can also check television and radio schedules and get tickets for BBC shows.

You could also try:
Channel 4, for listings and information, at:
http://www.channel4.com/

Sky Online, for all things satellite-related, at:
http://www.sky.co.uk/

myDigiGuide, for personalised TV and radio listings, at:
http://www.mydigiguide.com/

Music

dotmusic

`http://www.dotmusic.com/`

dotmusic is a UK e-zine (electronic magazine) with news, general and specialist charts, and information about many popular artists. You can listen to some of the top tracks and the Previews section has clips of forthcoming singles.

You could also try:

The Ultimate Band List, for information on over 100,000 artists and links to relevant web sites. Find it at:
`http://ubl.artistdirect.com/`

Jazz Online, which covers all styles of jazz music, "from traditional to straight-ahead to progressive to fusion to contemporary and more". Find it at:
`http://www.jazzonline.com/`

Classical.net, for information about composers, performers, recordings, genres and historical periods, at:
`http://www.classical.net/`

Magazines

National Geographic

http://www.nationalgeographic.com/

National Geographic has a fabulous web site, packed with photographs, maps, videos and interactive features. It isn't quite as convenient as the paper version – you can't read it on the train – but it's a lot more exciting. You can also go back to features from the last four or five years – something that isn't always easy with printed magazines.

You could also try:

Time, for political, business and entertainment news, at:
http://www.time.com/

The Economist, for all things financial, at:
http://www.economist.com/

Condé Nast London, for the on-line versions of *Vogue, GQ, Tatler, Vanity Fair, House and Garden, World of Interiors* and *Condé Nast Traveller*, at:
http://www.condenast.co.uk/

E-zines

Salon
http://www.salon.com/

The ease and speed with which web pages can be created has also spawned a host of web-only magazines or 'e-zines'.

Salon covers arts and entertainment, books, parenting, health, travel and technology. In addition to Sunday supplement-style features, it has interviews, news and media commentary, comic strips and 'table talk' forums. Salon concentrates on quality writing and is updated daily.

You could also try:

Slate, for news, politics and culture, at:
http://slate.msn.com/

The Onion, a satirical newspaper for over 18s, at:
http://www.theonion.com/

Women's Wire, for a female perspective on careers, money, style, entertainment and personal development, at:
http://www.womenswire.com/

Internet broadcasts

Yahoo! Broadcast
`http://broadcast.yahoo.com/`

Want to watch classic cartoons, movie trailers or NASA TV? Yahoo! Broadcasts lets you tune in over the Internet, using streaming audio and video (see page 45). Some broadcasts are archived so you can watch them whenever you want; others are only available live. You can also listen to music and audiobooks.

You could also try:

Web Events, Microsoft's catalogue of broadcasts, at:
`http://webevents.microsoft.com/`

AtomFilms, for cartoons and short films, at:
`http://www.atomfilms.com/`

Akoo.com, to track down radio stations that broadcast over the Internet. Find it at:
`http://www.akoo.com/`

Chat

Talk City

`http://www.talkcity.com/`

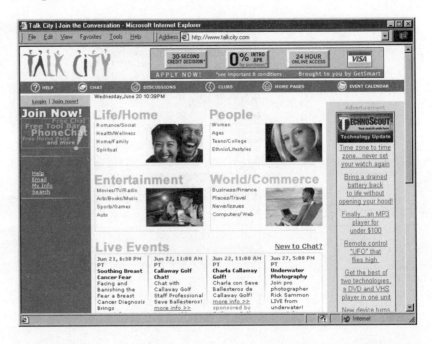

See page 114 for an explanation of Java.

Chat sites enable you to communicate with other Internet users in real time. Talk City is one of the best, partly because it uses a Java applet to keep the conversation flowing smoothly, and partly because its strict code of conduct deters troublemakers. You can talk about anything from music and movies to religion and politics, or play one of the fast-paced word games.

Sport

Football 365

http://www.football365.com/

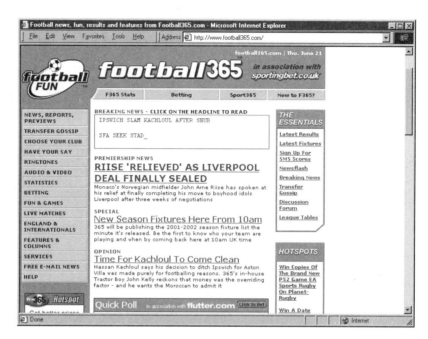

Football365 is a football site that's updated 365 days a year – hence the name. Its main attraction is a daily newspaper that you can have delivered by e-mail. The web site also has live scores from the English and Scottish leagues, breaking news, discussion forums and humorous columns.

You could also try:

CricInfo, "the home of cricket on the Internet". It's maintained by enthusiasts and has more statistics than you can shake a bat at. Find it at:

http://www-uk.cricket.org/

Golf.com, an extensive site with news, commentary and advice for those who like a good walk spoiled, at:

http://www.golf.com/

Formula1.com, an unofficial Formula 1 site, at:

http://www.formula1.com/

NBA.com

`http://www.nba.com/`

Having access to the Internet makes it easy to follow sports that aren't popular in the UK, such as baseball, basketball and American football. You can also get up-to-the-minute results from international events.

The NBA site enhances its news, previews, results and profiles with lots of multimedia extras, including sound samples and videos. You can also e-mail questions to selected players or join on-line chat sessions.

You could also try:

MLB.com, for Major League baseball, at:

`http://www.mlb.com/`

NFL.com, for the National (American) Football League, at:

`http://www.nfl.com/`

NHL.com, for the National (ice) Hockey League, at:

`http://www.nhl.com/`

Shopping

Amazon
http://www.amazon.co.uk/

See page 141 for advice about using your credit card to buy goods over the Internet.

Amazon is one of the most popular on-line retailers. Its UK branch offers over two million books, CDs, videos, DVDs, software titles and electronic gadgets. When you choose a book or CD, it lists other authors or artists bought by people who bought the item you've selected. Start with something you like and there's a good chance the links will lead you to something equally enjoyable. Many items have also been reviewed by previous customers.

You can also order books and CDs from the US branch (http://www.amazon.com/). They take longer to arrive, but you can purchase titles that aren't available in the UK.

You could also try:
CD Universe, for cut-price CDs, at:
http://www.cduniverse.com/

Black Star, for videos and DVDs, at:
http://www.blackstar.co.uk/

Tesco

`http://www.tesco.com/`

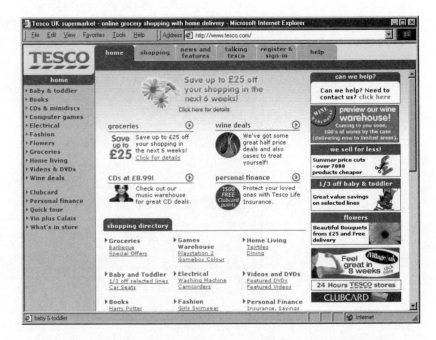

Books, CDs and videos will keep the family entertained, but sooner or later they'll get hungry. Save yourself the hassle of driving to the supermarket with Tesco's on-line store, which lets you pick out your groceries from an on-line catalogue, then have them delivered to your door. Check the web site to find out if your area is covered.

You could also try:

Sainsbury's to You, which also delivers in some areas, at `http://www.sainsburystoyou.co.uk/`

Iceland, which offers nationwide delivery, at: `http://www.iceland.co.uk/`

For details of many other on-line shops, including speciality food shops, visit 2020Shops, an on-line directory aimed at UK shoppers. Find it at: `http://www.2020shops.com/`

Travel

World Travel Guide
http://www.travel-guides.com/

An Internet version of the print publication often used by travel agents, the World Travel Guide is an encyclopædic reference to every country in the world (including Antarctica). It's short on atmosphere but long on facts, with information about accommodation, climate, essential documents and contact addresses as well as a general overview for each country.

You could also try:
Expedia, Microsoft's travel-booking site, at:
http://www.expedia.co.uk/

Lonely Planet On-line, for independent travellers, at:
http://www.lonelyplanet.com/

GORP, the Great Outdoor Recreation Pages, for active holidays. Find it at:
http://www.gorp.com/

Visit Britain
`http://www.visitbritain.com/`

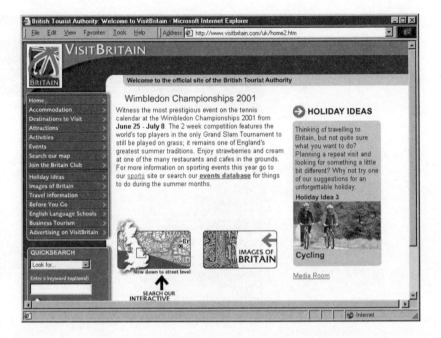

Find out what's worth seeing in the UK with Visit Britain, the British Tourist Authority's web site. It's relentlessly glowing, but does admit that you might need a waterproof. You can search for activities, events and places to visit or stay, and there's an excellent section on walking.

You could also try:

The RAC, which has an on-line route finder and will e-mail you details of roadworks and traffic jams. Find it at:
`http://www.rac.co.uk/`

Railtrack, for train times, at:
`http://www.railtrack.co.uk/`

National Express, for bus times and on-line bookings, at:
`http://www.nationalexpress.com/`

Multi Media Mapping, for maps of Great Britain, at:
`http://uk.multimap.com/`

Reference

Encyclopædia Britannica
http://www.britannica.com/

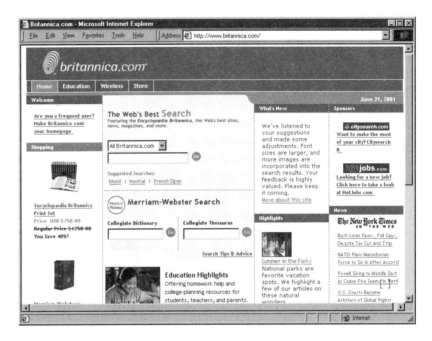

Check your facts by searching the on-line edition of the *Encyclopædia Britannica*. This is a great resource – it gives you access to all of the information in the printed version, without the effort of turning the pages, and also directs you to relevant web sites and on-line articles.

You could also try:

Encarta Online, the Internet version of Microsoft's multimedia encyclopædia, at:
http://encarta.msn.co.uk/

OneLook Dictionaries, which looks for your word in over 700 general and specialist dictionaries. Find it at:
http://www.onelook.com/

My Virtual Reference Desk, for pointers to thousands of reference sites, at:
http://www.refdesk.com/

Learn2

`http://www.learn2.com/`

Learn2 started out as a guide to the skills of everyday life: building fires, making beds, hosting dinner parties, throwing frisbees. It's now more interested in selling you on-line courses, mostly dealing with computer software, but if you head for the 'Free learning' section, you'll find hundreds of '2torials' on everything from arts and crafts to technology.

You could also try:

Delia Online, for recipes and advice from the queen of the boiled egg, Delia Smith. Find it at:
`http://www.deliaonline.com/`

Expertgardener, hosted by the ubiquitous Alan Titchmarsh and Charlie Dimmock, for help with your plants. Find it at:
`http://www.expertgardener.com/`

NHS Direct, for health information, at:
`http://www.nhsdirect.nhs.uk/`

UKonline

`http://www.ukonline.gov.uk/`

UKonline is a gateway to the multitude of government web sites. The 'Life episodes' section helps you find information relevant to particular events, such as having a baby or moving home. If you're looking for a specific organisation, go to the Quick Find section for A–Z lists. From here you can click through to the Foreign and Commonwealth Office web site, which has travel advice, or the Inland Revenue web site, for help with your tax return, and so on. There's also a 'Citizen space' section that explains how to vote and encourages you to contribute to government policy.

You could also try:

Want to know how much it costs to send an airmail letter to New Zealand? Ask Royal Mail, at:
`http://www.royalmail.co.uk/`

Want to check the price of a phone call? Try BT, at:
`http://www.bt.com/`

Science

NASA

http://www.nasa.gov/

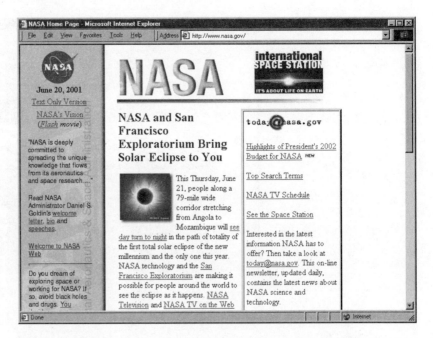

The NASA home page is the gateway to a vast collection of information about space and space exploration. Highlights include day-by-day reports from the shuttle, lots of historical information and a 'today@nasa.gov' section with the latest news. It can be hard to work out where your topic might be covered, but few institutions surpass NASA for quantity or quality of publicly available information.

You could also try:

The Why Files, for "the science behind the news", at:
http://whyfiles.org/

Discovery Channel Online, for a wide range of features with lots of pictures and interactive extras, at:
http://www.discovery.com/

New Scientist, for news, features, jobs and answers to questions such as, "Why do flying fish fly?" Find it at:
http://www.newscientist.com/

Computing: Reference

PC Webopaedia
http://www.pcwebopaedia.com/

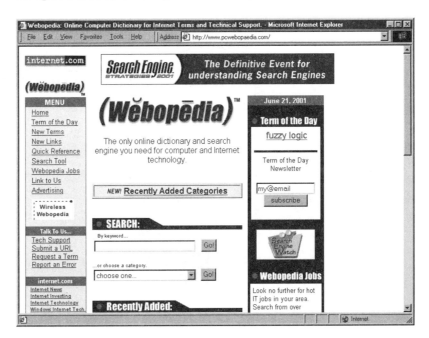

The PC Webopaedia specialises in explaining computer jargon. You can search for terms you've encountered in magazines, or browse through the categories to expand your knowledge. There's also a top-15 list of most requested terms so you can find out what is puzzling other Internet users. Many definitions have links to websites where you can get more in-depth coverage.

You could also try:
Whatis?com, another IT-specific encyclopedia, at:
http://whatis.techtarget.com/

The PC Technology Guide, which explains what the bits and bobs inside (or attached to) your PC actually do, at:
http://www.pctechguide.com/

Maximum PC, for reams of information from computer magazines produced by Future Publishing. Find it at:
http://www.maximumpc.co.uk/

Hardware

Dell
http://www.dell.co.uk/

Most computer manufacturers have extensive sites that showcase their products, provide technical support and even enable you to buy equipment on-line. They often have a lot more information than you'd find in an advertisement or get from a sales assistant.

Dell's web site is no exception: you can examine typical systems, or design your own and order it on-line. The technical support section has solutions to common problems and you can download the latest driver software.

You could also try:
If you're looking for a new modem, all the manufacturers have web sites. Try some of the following:

* 3Com/US Robotics, at http://www.3com.co.uk/

* S3/Diamond, at http://www.diamondmm.co.uk/

* Zoom/Hayes, at http://www.zoomtel.com/

Software

Adobe
`http://www.adobe.com/`

Graphics specialist Adobe has an excellent web site that provides detailed information about all its products. You can download tryout versions of most programs or get updates and extras for the ones you already own. The Support section has tutorials that help you master new techniques.

You could also try:
Corel, creator of CorelDRAW and Corel WordPerfect, at:
`http://www.corel.ca/`

Symantec, for utility and antivirus software, at:
`http://www.symantec.co.uk/`

Use Yahoo! (see page 76) or a search engine to track down other hardware and software companies.

Computer books

Computer Step

http://www.ineasysteps.com/

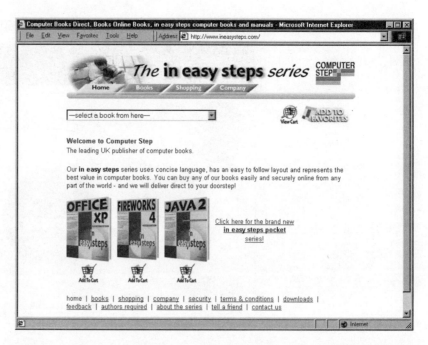

Find out about the other titles in this series from the on-line home of Computer Step, the leading British publisher of computer books.

You could also try:

Computer Manuals, a mail-order business that specialises in computer books, at:

http://www.compman.co.uk/

For more on Amazon, see also page 93.

Amazon, a bookshop but also a reference site about books and their authors with very strong search capabilities, at:

http://www.amazon.co.uk

Intermediate browsing

This chapter explains some of the tricks web authors use to make their pages more interesting. You'll learn how to use forms and frames and find out what is meant by buzz words such as 'Dynamic HTML' and 'Java'. The last two pages cover an older Internet service, FTP, that you may occasionally find useful.

Covers

Chapter Five

Forms

Forms enable you to enter keywords into search engines, fill out questionnaires and register for web sites. However, they aren't all dry and serious. They are also used for interactive gadgets such as automatic letter writers.

Forms are just like dialogue boxes, except the text boxes, drop-down lists, radio buttons and checkboxes are part of a web page. Once you have filled in the blanks, you click a button to send the data back to the web server. You'll get a response – another web page – a few seconds later.

Here's a form from Railtrack's web site (see page 96):

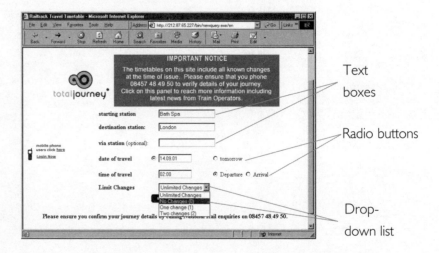

Text boxes

Radio buttons

Drop-down list

When you fill in your requirements and click Submit, you're given a list of suitable trains.

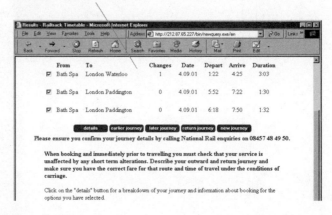

AutoComplete

Internet Explorer remembers all the things you've typed into forms and tries to anticipate your typing.

 AutoComplete only works when Internet Explorer knows what type of information a box should contain. It won't try to enter your name into an address box.

When you type a 'B' into the Destination box, Internet Explorer lists the 'B' place names you've entered previously. Click the correct one to fill in the box

starting station

destination station:

| B |
| Bath Spa |
| Bournemouth |
| Brighton |
| Bristol |

You can turn off AutoComplete if you don't find it helpful. You can also clear the list of words and start again.

1 Select Tools>Internet Options, then click the Content tab. Click the AutoComplete button

2 Deselect any or all of the AutoComplete options

3 Click Clear Forms if you want Internet Explorer to forget all the words you've typed into forms on web pages

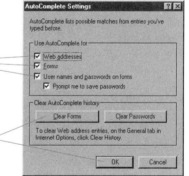

You can also delete individual items from the list associated with a particular text box.

To delete an item, perhaps because it's wrongly spelt, highlight it in the drop-down list and press Delete

starting station

destination station:

| B |
| Bath Spa |
| Bongor Regis |
| Bournemouth |
| Brighton |
| Bristol |

Site registration

Some of the large commercial sites require you to register for access. Usually the company wants to find out what kind of people visit the site so it can sell advertising. Knowing who you are also enables the web site to personalise its service. For example, it may display a list of pages that have been added since the last time you logged on.

On-line shops such as Amazon.co.uk (see page 93) may ask you to register when you make your first purchase. They keep your details on file so you can check out more quickly on subsequent visits. Instead of re-entering your address each time you buy something, you just confirm that the shop has the correct details.

Don't use the user name and password supplied by your Service Provider. Anyone who knows these details can use your Internet account, so keep them secret.

Registration involves filling in a form and selecting a user name and password. It's a good idea to write down your passwords and keep them somewhere safe, because you'll end up with more than you can possibly remember.

Registration

New to Amazon? Register Below

My name is: Mary Lojkine

My e-mail address: mary@lojkine.co.uk

Protect your information with a password
This will be your only Amazon.co.uk password.

Enter a new password: *********

Type it again: *********

Continue ▶

Internet Explorer may ask if it should remember the password for you. Whether this is a good idea depends on the nature of the web site and the number of people who use your computer. See Chapter 7 for more on passwords and Internet security.

Message boards

If you enjoy reading and contributing to message boards, you should also investigate Usenet newsgroups – see Chapter 9.

Message boards, sometimes known as forums, are like the letters page of a newspaper. The webmaster asks a question or proposes a topic, and anyone who passes by can have their say. All the responses are displayed on the web site.

CNN Interactive (see page 82) has a Community section with message boards where you can comment on everything from current events to religion, race relations, spaceflight and movies.

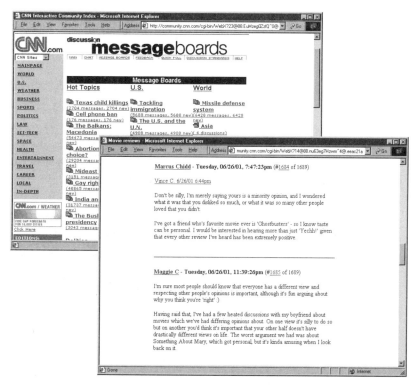

1 Once you've read all the messages, scroll to the bottom of the page and click Post

2 Fill in the form

3 Click POST MY MESSAGE to add your comments

Frames

Frames divide the main window into two or more 'panes' that can be scrolled or updated separately. They enable web designers to display several pages at once and are used to keep menus within easy reach.

Most pages that use frames have grey dividing bars between the sections, but it's possible for the designer to make the divisions invisible.

Clicking a link in one of the frames can change its contents, or change the contents of the other frames, or take you to a another web page. For example, About.com (see page 76) recommends sites on a wide range of subjects. When you click one of the links, Internet Explorer's main window is split into two frames. The bottom one displays the recommended web site. The top one enables you to return to About.com with a single click.

Top frame: About.com

Bottom frame: Electronic Telegraph (see page 81)

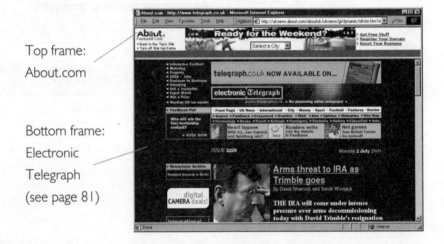

You can print the web page as on the screen, or frame by frame.

The selected frame is the one you've clicked in most recently.

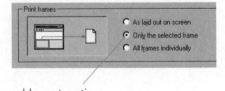

1 To print an individual frame, right-click within it. Select Print from the pop-up menu and choose the second layout option

2 Alternatively, left-click the frame, then go to File>Print Preview. Choose an option from the drop-down menu at the top

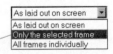

New windows

Web designers can also tell your browser to display a page for a few seconds, then load another one into the same window. This technique is used to create welcome screens and to redirect you when a site moves.

Clicking on a link sometimes opens a new copy of Internet Explorer instead of simply displaying the page. This isn't a mistake; the designer of the original site is hoping you'll explore the linked page, then close the new window and go back to where you were.

You can also choose to open a new window so you can compare two sites, take a detour or keep material on the screen for reference. If the Internet is very busy, you might even want to read a lengthy article in one window while you wait for images to download into another.

1 To open a second window, go to File>New>Window. Initially both windows display the same page, but you can use them independently

The more you try to do at once, the slower things get. Avoid downloading two image-heavy pages at once.

2 If you're browsing a list of recommended sites, such as this one prepared by the *New Scientist* team (see page 100), you can load them into new windows. Hold down Shift when you click the link, or right-click the link and select Open in New Window from the pop-up menu

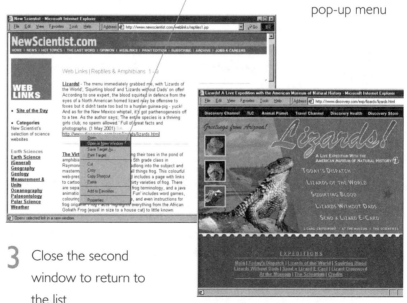

3 Close the second window to return to the list

Interactive web pages

Because web pages are displayed on a computer screen, rather than on paper, they can be designed to respond to your input. There are two ways to do this: the designer can add some extra instructions to the HTML document that describes the page, or they can incorporate a program that runs in a 'hole' in the page. Either way, your computer knows what to do when you point, click or type, so it isn't forever fetching new material from the web server. This speeds things up and makes browsing more fun.

JavaScript and VBScript

It's possible for a malicious programmer to use scripts to access private information or cause problems on your computer – see page 139 for more on this and similar hazards.

Scripts are sets of instructions that are included in the web page. You don't see them on the screen, but they tell Internet Explorer what to do when you click a button or enter some text. Scripts are used to display dialogue boxes, carry out simple calculations and add special effects such as scrolling messages. It's even possible to produce simple games and utilities.

The most popular scripting language is Netscape's JavaScript. Microsoft also uses its own language, Visual Basic Script (VBScript). From a web user's point of view, there isn't much difference between them, and standard installations of Internet Explorer support both languages.

There's nothing you can do about script errors except e-mail the designer of the site with details of the problem.

You're most likely to notice scripts when something goes wrong. If Internet Explorer encounters an instruction it doesn't understand, it displays an error message at the left-hand end of the Status bar.

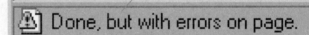

You can double-click the icon for a more detailed message, but it won't make much sense unless you're a programmer. Sometimes you can just ignore the error – you may be able to get all the information you want from the page, even though it isn't being displayed properly. However, if there are interactive elements, such as a form to fill out, they may not work properly.

Dynamic HTML

Dynamic HTML is a newish technology that was introduced in Internet Explorer 4 and is supported in Internet Explorer 6. It enables web authors to create more exciting pages that change as you browse.

Regular HTML enables authors to format their web pages (see page 38). Dynamic HTML uses scripting to add an interactive element – the formatting can change at a specified time, or in response to your mouse movements, mouse clicks and keystrokes. Items can appear or disappear, move around, change colour and so on. Previously the only way to change the design of a page was to load another one, but now the same page can be displayed several different ways. Because you don't have to sit through another download, the changes are almost instantaneous.

Additional Dynamic HTML features

Other features of Dynamic HTML include the ability to position images and other objects precisely. They can be overlapped, made transparent or moved around to animate the page. Pages that display data can include controls that enable you to sort, filter and otherwise manipulate the figures – without any further downloads. Again, this makes browsing faster and more interactive.

The downside of Dynamic HTML is that it's more difficult to work with than the regular sort, so you're more likely to encounter pages with errors. Also, as with many new web technologies, it's browser-specific. People with other browsers, or older versions of Internet Explorer, may not see all the features of a dynamic page.

You don't have to do anything special to experience effects created with Dynamic HTML. The capability is built into Internet Explorer, so you'll see them automatically.

Java

Although they have similar names, Java and JavaScript don't have much in common – they don't even come from the same company.

Java is a programming language developed by Sun Microsystems. It enables web authors to write small programs, or 'applets', that can be embedded in web pages. They are downloaded along with the text and images, slotted into the page and run automatically. Java is used to create animations, games and utilities.

The thing that makes Java special – and the reason for all the hype about it – is that a single Java program can run on many different types of computer. It's a two-part system: as well as the programs, you have the Java Virtual Machine, which is built into your browser. The programs are the same for everyone, but the Virtual Machine is specific to a particular type of computer. It acts as an interpreter, converting the standard code into something your computer understands.

When you download a page with an attached applet, you'll see a blank rectangle, usually grey, in the area the applet uses. After a few seconds, the rectangle is replaced by the animation or game (look out for an 'Applet Started' message in the Status bar).

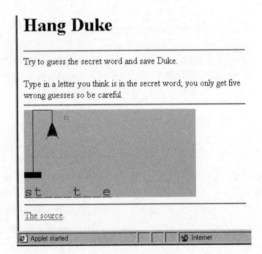

The difference between Java applets and the technologies discussed on the previous two pages is that applets are downloaded separately from the document that describes the page, whereas scripts and Dynamic HTML are part of that document. However, you don't need to know how an effect was achieved to enjoy it.

For more on Java, or to see some applets in action, visit the Sun Microsystems web site at:
`http://java.sun.com/`

File Transfer Protocol

As well as supporting HTTP (HyperText Transfer Protocol – the system that's used to transfer web pages from the Internet to your computer), Internet Explorer enables you to use an older technology called FTP (File Transfer Protocol).

As the name suggests, FTP is a way of moving files from one computer to another. FTP sites are simply huge libraries of files, organised much like your hard disk. Internet Explorer shows you one folder (directory) at a time.

The FTP site at `ftp://ftp.demon.net/` *belongs to Demon Internet, a UK-based Internet Service Provider. It contains a wide range of files, including programs for many different types of computer. For PC software, go into the 'pub' folder, then look in 'ibmpc' or 'simtelnet'.*

1   To open an FTP site, type the URL into the Address bar. It should begin with `ftp://` (you may have to add this bit yourself). Press Enter or click Go

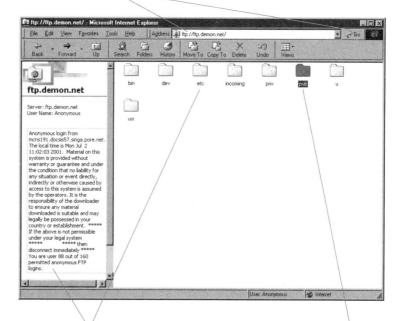

2   Internet Explorer displays a message on the left and a list of folders and files on the right

3   Look for welcome, readme or index files to find out how the site is organised. Double-click them to display their contents. If there are no instructions, look for a 'pub' or 'public' folder

4 Double-click the folder you want to open. To go back to the original one, click the Up button on the Windows Explorer-style toolbar that replaces the Standard buttons

If you don't see this kind of 'files and folders' display when you try to access an FTP site, you need to install the Internet Explorer Browsing Enhancements component – see page 118. You can change the style of the display using the View menu – select Large Icons (for the displays shown here), Small Icons, List or Details.

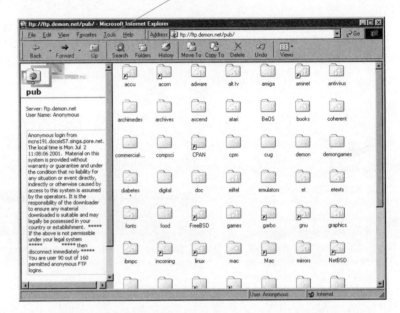

5 When you find an interesting file, double-click on it, then follow the instructions on page 46 to download it on to your hard disk

Internet Explorer's FTP facilities are useful when a link from a website unexpectedly takes you to an FTP site so you can download a file. However, they're very limited compared to those of specialist FTP programs. If you plan to spend a lot of time exploring FTP sites, or have created your own website and need to upload it using FTP, get a proper FTP program, such as:

Cute FTP, from GlobalSCAPE at:
`http://www.cuteftp.com/`

WS_FTP, from Ipswitch at:
`http://www.ipswitch.com/`

Extending your browser

This chapter explains how to teach Internet Explorer new tricks. It shows you how to update your software and install ActiveX controls. It also covers the most popular add-ons.

Covers

Chapter Six

Installing extra components

When you first installed Internet Explorer, you probably didn't install all the extra bits and pieces that come with it. Most people start by selecting the 'Typical installation' option and don't worry about the more obscure components until they've got to grips with the basics.

It's easy to go back and add to your installation if you find you've missed something vital or someone recommends that you try one of the add-on programs.

If you need one of the optional components to view a web site properly, Internet Explorer prompts you to install it. Click the Download button to get it straight away.

I Go to the Start menu and select Settings>Control Panel. Double-click Add/Remove Programs

2 Select Microsoft Internet Explorer 6 and Internet Tools from the list of programs and click the Add/Remove button

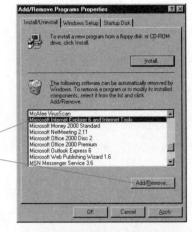

3 Select the 'Add a component' option and click OK

If you got your copy of Internet Explorer from Microsoft's web site, Add/Remove will assume you want to download the extra components.

4 You may be prompted to insert your CD

5 The setup program (see pages 18–20) runs again. Select the components you want to install

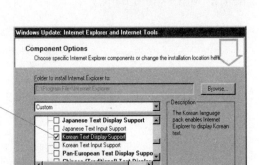

Updating your software

When you buy software in a shop, you're buying a finished product. You take it home, open the box, install it and that's that – nothing changes until the next version comes out.

Internet Explorer evolves more gradually. Each version is preceded by 'preview' or 'beta' releases that let experienced browsers get a glimpse of the future. Eventually a 'final' version is released, but the story doesn't end there. Microsoft produces updates and extras every few months, so the software on your CD may not be the latest version.

BEWARE *Preview versions of Internet Explorer are often very unstable and are not recommended for beginners. Wait for the final version, then upgrade it each time an update appears. Updates fix any security problems that have been discovered (see page 139) and should work a little better.*

1 To find out whether Microsoft has released new software, go to the Start menu and select Windows Update. When the web site is displayed, click the Product Updates link

2 Windows Update checks to see what software is installed on your computer

3 Internet Explorer displays a list of components you can add. Select the ones you want and click the Download button

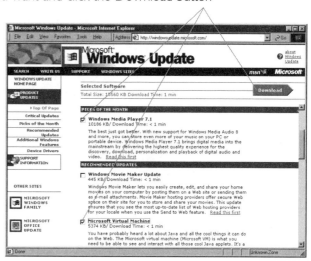

4 Follow the on-screen instructions to download and install the new software. Usually this is a one-step process and you just have to click OK at the end

ActiveX Controls

ActiveX Controls are small pieces of software that add extra features to Internet Explorer. They're often used to handle multimedia files, such as new types of sound and video file, animations and 360-degree panoramas.

You can think of ActiveX Controls as the electronic equivalent of extra blades for your food processor. Each time you want to do something new, you download the extra software that enables Internet Explorer to slice, dice, shred and otherwise process the data. Some of these add-ons are produced by Microsoft, but most come from other companies.

Most ActiveX Controls are installed automatically. When you visit a page that requires a new one, Internet Explorer locates and downloads it (see opposite). You get the option to abort the installation, but otherwise everything is done for you. You shouldn't even have to disconnect from the Internet.

Some add-ons have to be installed by hand (see page 122). Once you've checked that the software is compatible with Internet Explorer, you download the version for your operating system, then log off and run the setup program.

Despite the confusing terminology, installing add-ons is actually quite straightforward. If you need an ActiveX Control to view a web page, Internet Explorer should install it for you. If it doesn't, you probably need to install the software yourself, in which case there'll be a link to a site that you can download it from.

Automatic installation

The great thing about ActiveX Controls is that they are very easy to install. When you encounter a page that requires a new one, Internet Explorer downloads it automatically.

1 Internet Explorer displays a security warning (see page 136) and asks if you want to install the ActiveX Control

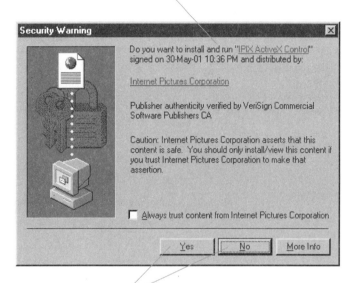

2 Click Yes if you have confidence in the company that published the software, or No to abort the installation

3 If you click Yes, the Control is installed. Internet Explorer is able to make use of it straight away, so you'll see or hear the additional material in a few seconds.

Manual installation

If you have to install an add-on by hand, you'll be directed to the Home Page of the company that supplies it. For example, sites that use RealAudio normally provide a 'Get RealPlayer' button that takes you to the RealNetworks Home Page.

Check the system requirements for an add-on before you download it. Note also that plug-ins that work with older versions of Internet Explorer don't always work with version 6.

1 You'll probably need to enter your details in a form. This enables the web site to supply the correct version

2 Download the file, just as you would any other program file (see page 46). Make sure you know what it's called and where you've put it

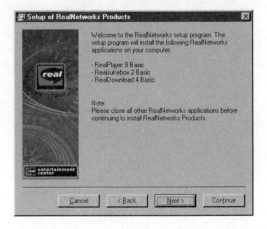

3 Once you've disconnected from the Internet, locate the file using Windows Explorer or My Computer. Double-click it to start the setup routine and install the add-on

Shockwave and Flash

Shockwave, Flash and RealPlayer (see overleaf) are the three most useful add-ons. They enable you to view some of the most exciting sites on the web, so most people have them.

Shockwave and Flash add visual pizazz to the web. The Flash player is used to display animations and special effects. Its more sophisticated sibling, the Shockwave player, gives you access to multimedia presentations and games.

Flash animations are very compact, download quickly and can include interactive elements, such as buttons that react when you point or click. They're often used to add movement to the main page of a web site.

Macromedia's Shockwave site catalogues the best 'shocked' sites and is great fun to explore. Find it at:

http://www.shockwave.com

Shockwave movies are more complex and take longer to download. They can combine text, graphics, animation, digital video, sound and interactive elements. You're most likely to find them on entertainment sites.

Both players are produced by Macromedia. Find out more from: http://www.macromedia.com/

RealPlayer

See page 45 to find out how streaming works.

RealPlayer is produced by streaming-sound pioneer RealNetworks. It enables you to listen to RealAudio sound and watch RealVideo video, both of which play as they download. There's no waiting around – you start hearing or seeing the clip a few seconds after you click the link.

RealAudio is often used to transmit radio shows, news bulletins and special events over the Internet. Sound quality deteriorates when the Internet is very busy, but generally it's pretty good, especially for voice broadcasts. Music doesn't transmit as well, but you can recognise your favourite songs. Sites that sell CDs often have RealAudio clips of sample tracks so you can check that you're buying the right disk.

RealVideo gives you pictures as well as sound, but doesn't work quite as well over dial-up connections. The pictures are small and fuzzy and it can be hard to work out what's going on.

However, there's something exciting about using the Internet to tune into a television signal from the other side of the world. Use the Channels and Radio menus to find something to watch or listen to, or visit the RealGuide web site for details of special broadcasts.

Find it at:
`http://realguide.real.com/`

Get RealPlayer from the RealNetworks web site at:
`http://www.real.com/`

QuickTime

The QuickTime player enables you to play video clips recorded in Apple's QuickTime format. It can also handle video, sound and image files saved in many other formats.

QuickTime movies may play in a separate window or be integrated into the web page – it depends on the web designer's wishes.

There's a lot of overlap between Windows Media Player (supplied with Windows), RealPlayer and the QuickTime player. They all play most types of video clip and they all support streaming. However, some clips only play in the 'correct' player, so you'll probably end up with all three on your hard disk.

The main reason for installing the QuickTime player is that the format has become popular for movie trailers. The Apple web site has a section devoted to QuickTime promos for new films, at:
`http://www.apple.com/trailers/`

Other attractions include QuickTime TV, which is used for Internet broadcasts, and QuickTime VR (Virtual Reality). QuickTime VR files are similar to IPIX images (see overleaf).

Download the QuickTime player from:
`http://www.apple.com/quicktime/`

IPIX

The IPIX viewer, produced by Interactive Pictures Corporation, enables you to step inside 360-by-360-degree panoramic images. It creates the illusion that you are standing in the middle of a scene, able to spin round and look in any direction. You can also zoom in or out, and sometimes there are hotspots that take you on to other images. IPIX images are used to show you the interiors of houses, hotels and museums, and also to take you to places you're unlikely to visit personally, such as the International Space Station.

Find out more from the IPIX Home Page at:
`http://www.ipix.com/`

Use the IPIX viewer to explore sets from popular police drama The Bill at:

http://www.thebill.com/

There are several other formats for panoramic images. The one you're most likely to encounter is QuickTime VR, which requires Apple's QuickTime movie player (see previous page). Find out more from:
`http://www.apple.com/quicktime/qtvr/`

Beatnik

The Beatnik player is an audio plug-in from Beatnik Incorporated. It is used to create 'sonified' web sites with interactive audio – music and sound effects that are triggered by your mouse.

RMF files are similar to MIDI files, but more sophisticated. The player can also handle regular MIDI files – which, like RMF files, specify the pitch, duration and volume of each note.

MIDI is short for Musical Instrument Digital Interface, a standard that lays down rules for controlling soundcards and synthesisers.

Most sound files are a recording of an actual performance. However, Beatnik files (also known as Rich Music Format or RMF files) are different. They tell the Beatnik player which instrument to simulate, what notes to play, for how long, and at what volume. You can think of them as the electronic equivalent of sheet music.

If a piece of music requires an unusual instrument, such as a gamelan, the Beatnik player downloads a short sample, then manipulates it to create the required notes. It can produce a lengthy song from a relatively small file, because most of the work is done on your computer.

Beatnik also reacts to your mouse movements and clicks, providing audible feedback. As you move the mouse pointer over each of the graphics shown below, you hear an appropriate sound.

Sonified Graphics

Imagine surfing to a web site where not only do you see text & graphic images, you also hear auditory feedback in response to your mouse movements and clicks. High-quality, low-bandwidth audio can be added to any web page using standard JavaScript.

At the time of writing Beatnik had not been updated to work with Internet Explorer 6, but hopefully there'll be a new version by now. Check the website for the latest news.

The player is easier to use than it is to explain, and you'll enjoy finding out what it can do. Download it from:
`http://www.beatnik.com/`

Acrobat

Adobe's Acrobat Reader is a page-viewing tool that enables you to browse documents saved as PDF (Portable Document Format) files. This format preserves the layout of a document as well as its content, so the copy you see on your screen looks the same as a printed copy of the original file. You can't edit the PDF version, but you can read or print it – even if you don't have the DTP program or word processor used to create the document.

PDF files are used to distribute electronic versions of brochures and forms. They look good and print out well, so they're a popular choice when presentation is important. They also make it easy for companies to put existing documents on the web.

Once you've installed Acrobat Reader, PDF files can be viewed from within Internet Explorer. The two programs work together, displaying both sets of tools in the same window. This means you can jump from a web page to a PDF file, or vice versa, without switching applications.

Lost your manual? Some companies put electronic ones on their web sites. For example, you can find PDF versions of the manuals for Nikon digital cameras and scanners at:

http://www.nikon-euro.com/

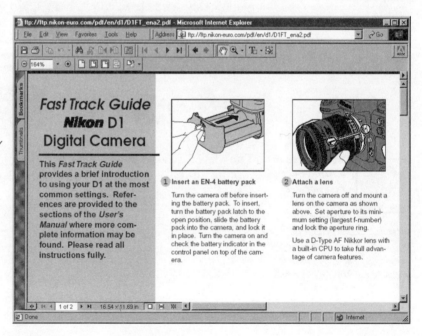

Find out more from Adobe's web site at:
`http://www.adobe.com/`

Menus, buttons and bars

You can also install add-ons that give you new toolbars, buttons, menu options or Explorer bars, enabling you to do more with your browser. These add-ons were originally known as PowerToys, and then as Web Accessories. Currently they don't have a snappy name but the technology is still supported. If developers want to add new features to Internet Explorer, they can.

Extra menu options

When Internet Explorer 5 was launched, Microsoft's programmers created a set of eight Web Accessories. Some of them added new menu options; others created extra buttons on the Links bar. These tools are not supposed to be used with Internet Explorer 6, but you'll come across people who still have them installed. In their day they were very popular and it's easy to forget that they weren't part of a 'normal' copy of Internet Explorer. The tools were:

1   Open Frame in New Window: select any frame (see page 110) and display it in a window of its own.

2   Quick Search: let you select your favourite engine when searching from the Address bar (see page 67).

3   Zoom In/Zoom Out: for a closer view of images.

4   Image Toggler: turned off the images so web pages downloaded more quickly.

5   Text Highlighter: for marking interesting passages on long web pages.

6   Web Search: lets you select a word from a web page, then send it to the default search engine as a keyword.

7   Links List: listed all the links on the current page.

8   Image List: a tool for web designers. It displayed the images from the current page, with their sizes in bytes and pixels.

It's possible that Microsoft will release a new set of tools designed for Internet Explorer 6. For more information, check out the Web Accessories section of its website, at (no spaces):

```
http://www.microsoft.com/windows/ie/
previous/webaccess/
```

Extra toolbars

There are several add-ons that give you a new toolbar with additional tools. For example, search engine Google (see page 77) offers a toolbar that makes it easy to search the web, an individual web site or the current page.

Sometimes you can display the extra toolbar at the bottom of the main window, rather than the top. To do this, go to View> Explorer Bars. If your toolbar appears on the list, select it.

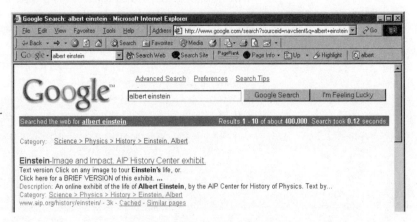

For more on AI Roboform, visit the following web site at:

http://www.roboform.com/

Another example is AI Roboform, a form-filling utility created by Siber Systems. Once you've told it personal details such as your name and address, it can fill in any forms you encounter on web sites. All you have to do is click the Fill Forms button.

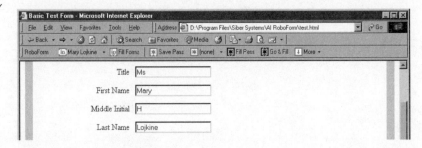

Once you've installed extra toolbars, you turn them on and off from the pop-up menu (see page 29).

Right-click on an empty section of any of your toolbars and select or deselect the new one

Extra buttons

Some add-ons give you extra buttons as well as (or instead of) an entire toolbar. When you install AI Roboform, you not only get a new toolbar, but also three buttons that you can display alongside the standard ones. The extra buttons enable you to access AI Roboform's main features even when its toolbar is turned off.

1 To display extra buttons, right-click on an empty section of the Standard buttons. Select Customize.

2 The new buttons appear in the 'Available toolbar buttons' list. Follow the instructions on page 30 to add them to the Standard buttons.

Extra Explorer bars

Add-on Explorer bars are displayed at the left-hand side of the Internet Explorer window, or across the bottom. Some give you access to search engines and other on-line tools, while others display up-to-the-minute headlines, sports results and stock quotes as you browse. Once you've opened an Explorer bar, it stays open, no matter where you go on the web. Its information and services are always accessible.

The New York Times' Explorer bar offers news headlines and stock quotes. It also has shortcuts to the main sections of the paper's web site (see page 82).

iMarkup from iMarkup Solutions Incorporated is an annotation utility that enables you to attach notes to web pages. When you return to the page, your note reappears. It's the Internet equivalent of adding sticky notes to a reference book or report.

...cont'd

For more information about iMarkup or to download a trial version, visit the site at:

http://www.imarkup.com/

iMarkup's tools appear in an Explorer bar down the left-hand side of the main window. It also gives you an extra toolbar, a button to add to the Standard Buttons, and some menu options.

Extra toolbar   Extra button

Extra Explorer bar   Extra menu options

You'll see other add-ons mentioned in Internet magazines, or come across them as you browse the web. You can also visit a search engine (see page 77) and search for 'Explorer bar'.

Internet security

This chapter discusses the vexing questions of Internet security and on-line pornography. You'll learn how to avoid viruses, hackers and scams, protect your privacy and make the Internet safe for children.

Covers

Chapter Seven

Security

When you connect your computer to the Internet, you're able to access a great wealth of information. Unfortunately, you also expose your own data to hackers and viruses.

The prospect of losing important information makes many people dubious about purchasing a modem. In reality, though, your files are more likely to be destroyed by errors and hardware failures, and you probably do a dozen potentially unsafe things every day. There are risks associated with using the Internet, and it's a good idea to be aware of them, but it isn't difficult to keep them at a manageable level. Internet Explorer's Security zones (see page 139) make it easy to select sensible security settings for several types of web site.

If you use your computer to store information that is confidential, irreplaceable or valuable to others, consult a security expert before connecting it to the Internet. On the other hand, if losing the data on your hard disk would merely be irritating and inconvenient, you can protect yourself against most types of attack by making regular backups of important files. In either case, following the advice given over the next few pages will reduce the chances of anything going wrong.

Viruses

Note that there are the following types of malicious program:

- viruses
- worms
- Trojan horses

A virus attaches itself to other programs. A worm can replicate independently and doesn't need to attach itself to a program. Trojans don't replicate – they just cause damage if you make the mistake of running them.

A computer virus is a small piece of program code that attaches itself to other programs. When you run the infected program, the virus copies itself to another program or causes your computer to do something untoward. Some are just irritating, but others may damage or destroy your files.

You can only 'catch' a computer virus by running an infected program. As well as checking all the software you download, you should be wary of programs attached to e-mails and newsgroup messages. If you aren't sure how to identify program files (it gets harder every year), be suspicious of anything sent to you by a stranger. You can't trust your friends, either. If you get a message that seems out of character, don't open any attached files. Check with the friend first – the message may have been sent without their knowledge.

Protect yourself by investing in antivirus software and updating it regularly. It's also a good idea to establish a schedule for backing up files that contain important information or would be difficult to replace. Download software from large, well-managed file archives or directly from the company concerned.

Software that is incomplete, badly written or simply incompatible with one of your other applications can also upset your computer. The more you download, the more important it is to make backups.

Macro viruses

Files that may contain macros, such as Microsoft Word and Excel documents, can also carry viruses. Macro viruses are a particularly sneaky development, because the files they infect don't look like programs. They've become very common in recent years and even documents from reputable sources may be infected.

Recent versions of Word and Excel can protect you against macro viruses. If you're using a very old version that doesn't have this option, use a virus checker on any Word or Excel files before you open them.

To avoid macro viruses in Word or Excel, go to Tools>Macro> Security. Click the Security Level tab and select 'High' or 'Medium'. In older versions, go to Tools>Options, click the General tab and select 'Macro virus protection'.

Authenticode

It's impossible to make the most of the web without downloading lots of add-ons (see Chapter 6). However, it's difficult to be sure whether you're downloading a useful utility that will enhance your web browsing or a rogue program designed to attack your system. There's also the risk that a genuine program might have been sabotaged somewhere along its journey.

To counter these fears, Microsoft has developed a system called Authenticode that helps you decide whether you can safely install an add-on. It enables publishers to add a 'digital signature' to their software, so you can be sure of its origin. These signatures are the on-line equivalent of the holograms attached to Microsoft's software boxes – they demonstrate that the application is genuine.

The digital signature takes the form of a certificate that verifies the identity of the publisher of the program. The presence of a certificate also proves that the program hasn't been tampered with along the way.

Authenticode works for programs that are installed from within Internet Explorer. If you save an installation file on to your hard disk instead of selecting Open to run it straight away, you won't see the certificate.

When you download an upgrade or add-on, you'll be shown its certificate before it is installed. If it's unsigned, you'll get a warning message instead

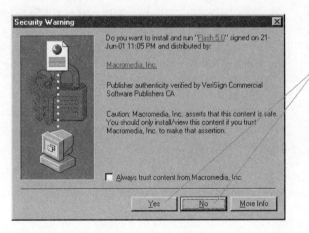

2 Click Yes to continue the installation or No if you don't have confidence in the publisher

Virus hoaxes

There are a number of virus hoaxes that do the rounds by e-mail. The best-known example is a message that tells you not to open messages with 'Good Times' in the subject line. Doing so will delete your files and destroy your processor – or so the story goes.

This is nonsense, because you cannot catch a virus from a text-only e-mail message. However, the Good Times hoax is almost as troublesome as a real virus, because people waste a lot of time sending the message to their friends, calling their systems manager and so on.

If you receive a warning that you think might be a hoax, don't pass it on 'just in case'. You'll get your less knowledgeable friends worried over nothing, and those with more experience will think you're gullible.

How can you tell whether a virus warning is a hoax? You should be suspicious of any warning message that:

1   Contains lots of exclamation marks!!!!!

2   Tells you something dreadful will happen if you open an e-mail message with a particular title.

3   Promises total destruction of your hard disk, your processor, your entire computer, your home…

4   References a technical-sounding organisation you've never heard of and can't find on the web.

5   Encourages you to pass it on to all your friends.

You can find out whether your message is a well-known hoax by looking it up on one of the following web sites:

CIAC Internet Hoaxes, at:
`http://hoaxbusters.ciac.org/`

Symantec's Anti-virus Resource Center, at:
`http://www.symantec.com/avcenter/`

Chain letters and scams

It's an unfortunate fact of Internet life that the ease with which you can send e-mail or create web pages encourages some people to abuse these services. You shouldn't believe everything you read on the web, and you shouldn't take every e-mail message seriously.

Chain letters

There are two sorts of chain letter. One type has a list of names and promises you enormous wealth if you send a small sum of money to the person at the top. You're then supposed to add your name and redistribute the message. It's mathematically impossible for most of these schemes to pay off, and they're probably illegal. Many Service Providers will close your account if they catch you forwarding this kind of junk.

The other type promises you good luck if you forward it to all your friends, and bad luck if you don't. Some of these messages are very unpleasant, and you should delete them. You are not doing your friends any favours by sending them messages that threaten all sorts of dire consequences if they 'break the chain'.

The Craig Shergold story is an urban legend – a tale that keeps being told, regardless of its veracity. You can find many more in The AFU & Urban Legends Archive, at (no spaces):

http://www.urbanlegends. com/

There are also some well-meaning chain letters that ask you to send cards to a sick child – usually Craig Shergold, a boy with cancer – who is trying to get into *The Guinness Book of Records*. There's actually some truth to this story, which dates back to the late 1980s. However, Shergold got his record, had an operation and got on with his life, so there's no need to send a card. The organisations mentioned in the letter receive quite enough unwanted mail already.

Scams

There are numerous scams circulating the Internet, some of which are quite convincing. Be suspicious of anything that sounds too good to be true, and learn to recognise the most common tricks.

Internet ScamBusters is a good source of information and advice, and issues regular newsletters. Find it at:
`http://www.scambusters.org/`

Other hazards

If someone reports a serious weakness in Internet Explorer, Microsoft releases a 'patch' – a small upgrade that fixes the problem. Get the latest ones from its website, at (no spaces):

http://www.microsoft.com/ windows/ie/download/ default.asp

Internet Explorer's warnings are just that – warnings. It isn't telling you that what you want to do will cause a problem, just that it might. It's up to you to decide whether there's genuine cause for concern.

Almost all the things that make web sites interesting can also be abused to cause you problems. Scripts, Java applets and ActiveX Controls can all potentially be used to attack your computer, although so far the risks seem more theoretical than actual. People keep discovering different ways these technologies can be used to steal passwords or monitor your browsing, but the reports are coming from researchers rather than victims.

Trying to make an accurate assessment of the risks to your computer will give you a headache. Most on-line activities are potentially dangerous, but then so are most kitchen implements. The problem is compounded by the fact that your confidence will vary from site to site. You probably trust well-known companies to produce 'safe' web sites, but you might have a few qualms about the skills and intentions of a complete unknown.

To make things simpler, Internet Explorer provides four security settings – High, Medium, Medium-Low and Low. These settings cover all kinds of interactive content, plus file downloads and communication with insecure sites (see page 141). The High setting prevents you from downloading anything that could cause problems, keeping you safe but cutting you off from some of the more exciting aspects of the web. Medium is less severe: it bans some unsafe content and warns you about the rest. Medium-Low is the same, but without the warnings. It's a rejigged Medium setting for people who always ignore the warning messages. Finally, the Low setting enables anyone and everyone to mess with your computer.

Rather than making you use the same setting for every site you visit, Internet Explorer divides the Internet into four 'zones': Local Intranet (your company's internal network), Trusted, Internet and Restricted. Initially all web sites are in the Local Intranet or Internet zones (if you connect with a modem, they'll all be in the Internet zone). As you gain experience, you can add sites to the Trusted ('safe') and Restricted ('unsafe') zones. Internet Explorer will be more lenient or more protective when you visit those sites.

It only takes a couple of minutes to decide what level of protection you require and select an appropriate security setting. You can then let Internet Explorer do the worrying and get on with browsing the web.

1 To choose a security setting, go to Tools>Internet Options, then click the Security tab

2 Choose the Internet zone

If you're a security expert, you can fine-tune your security setting by clicking Custom. This option enables you to select the types of content you want to allow and avoid.

3 Move the slider to High (at the top) to eliminate potential hazards

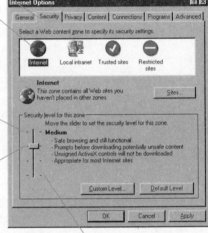

4 Medium security exposes you to some risks, but enables you to enjoy interactive web content. You receive warnings about potential hazards. Medium-Low is the same, but without the warning messages

5 Low security is only recommended for sites on your (adequately protected) company network

If you're using Internet Explorer at work, your systems manager may have added some sites to the Trusted and Restricted zones. If not, it's up to you to decide which sites fall in these categories.

1 To add a site to the Trusted or Restricted zone, click the appropriate icon, then click Sites. Enter the address and click Add. Click OK to finish

On-line shopping

As well as protecting the data on your computer, you need to think about the information you transmit over the Internet. You probably don't care whether the keywords you submit to search engines can be intercepted (and it's unlikely a hacker would bother), but you won't want to share your credit-card number with other Internet users.

Do not enter your credit-card number into insecure forms or include it in e-mail messages. The same rules apply to any other confidential information.

Internet shopping is fairly safe as long as you stick to reputable companies that use secure servers to collect your details. When you're connected to a secure server, all the data you send is encrypted to protect it from eavesdroppers. There are several ways to identify a secure server:

1 Internet Explorer normally informs you that you're opening a secure connection

2 Secure addresses begin with `https://` rather than `http://`

3 A padlock icon appears at the right-hand end of the Status bar

If a web site uses frames (see page 110), it's hard to tell whether it is secure. Right-click within the frame that holds the order form and select Properties to check the status of the connection.

4 Double-click the padlock to see the site's security certificate

5 Internet Explorer will display another warning message when you leave the secure server

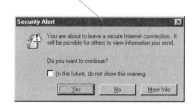

You may have to pay duty and VAT on items bought from overseas web sites. The Customs and Excise publication 'Notice 143: A Guide for International Post Users' explains the rules. Find it on the Customs and Excise web site at:

http://www.hmce.gov.uk/

You can also protect yourself by sticking to a few simple rules when you're shopping on-line.

1   Give your money to companies you're familiar with, or whose sites have been recommended by people you trust.

2   Look around before you buy. Can you find the company's street address and phone number? How much will delivery cost? Will the company take your goods back if there's a problem? Good shopping sites provide plenty of information about their services.

3   If you aren't sure about a company, request a catalogue or make contact over the phone.

4   Print out details of your order (see page 51), and keep any confirmation e-mails you receive.

5   Check your credit-card statement each month and make sure you can account for all the purchases.

6   Choose a different password for each shopping site, and keep these passwords secret. Many sites keep a record of your details, which is very convenient if you make regular purchases. However, it also enables anyone who knows your password to enjoy an afternoon's shopping at your expense. See opposite for more on passwords.

Internet shopping can save you time and money and enable you to buy things you wouldn't normally get in the shops. Don't be put off by all these warnings – if you shop sensibly, it may be safer than walking down the street with a bulging wallet in your back pocket.

Passwords

Passwords are the bane of Internet users' lives. If you aren't thinking one up for a site you've just discovered, you're trying to recall the one you chose last week.

Choosing passwords

There are two common ways for someone to break your password: they can guess it, or they can use a program that works through a dictionary, trying every word. Try to choose passwords that are immune to both types of attack. Don't use your name, your partner's name, your date of birth or any other easily obtainable information. Where possible, choose a mixture of numbers and letters, and make each password at least six characters long.

Remembering passwords

Never reveal the password that you use to connect to the Net to anyone you meet on-line, even if they claim that they work for your Service Provider and need your details to prevent a problem with your account. Anyone who asks for this information is up to no good.

If you log on to the Internet from home and lead a fairly blameless life, choosing good passwords is often less important than finding some way to remember the ones you've already picked.

Internet Explorer can remember many passwords for you. It doesn't do this by default; instead, it asks if you want this feature turned on the first time you type a password into a web site. If you click Yes, it will offer to remember each password you enter.

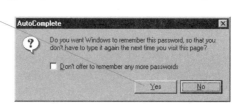

You may want to use this feature for sites where your password simply gives you access. It's less of a good thing on shopping sites, especially if your computer is configured to remember your log-on password (see page 23).

> To turn this feature off, go to Tools>Internet Options. Click the Content tab, then click the AutoComplete button. Deselect the 'User names and passwords' option. You can also clear the password list

Privacy

As you browse the web, you'll notice that a lot of sites want to know who you are, where you live, how old you are, what sort of music you like, and so on. Sometimes a web site has a good reason for collecting this data. A weather site needs to know where you are to provide the correct forecast, and an on-line shop needs your address to deliver your goods.

A weather site is just a convenient example. Weather sites are no worse than any other type of website.

Sometimes there's another reason for collecting personal data: marketing. If a weather site wants to know what kind of music you listen to, it might be planning to pass on your details to companies that sell CDs or concert tickets. The result is a load of junk mail from companies you've never heard of. You don't recall giving them your details because you didn't – they bought them from the weather site.

Another concern is consolidation of personal information. Suppose one site wants your address, another site asks for your date of birth, and a third one wants your mother's maiden name. If they share their information, they can build up a detailed profile.

Cookies

Some of the information you enter into on-line forms ends up on your hard disk, in a file called a 'cookie'. Here's how it works:

If a web page includes an advert, the advertiser may also create a cookie on your hard disk. They can use it to keep track of the pages you've visited or the adverts you've seen.

Suppose you visit a weather site and enter your name (John) and postcode (EC1). The site tells your web browser to record the information in a cookie file, which is stored in your Windows folder. Next time you visit the site, it asks your browser to send back the information from the cookie. It then creates a customised web page with a personalised message: 'Hello John, it's raining in London, so don't forget your umbrella.'

The advantage of this system is that you get the forecast you want, straight away. The disadvantage is that the site knows who you are. If you start checking the weather in Spain or Greece, it might give your e-mail address to a travel agent.

Reputable sites have privacy statements that explain what they do with the information they collect. Once you've read the statement, you can decide whether to enter your details.

Privacy settings

Reading privacy statements is tedious, so Internet Explorer gives you an alternative. It can accept or reject cookies automatically, based on your predefined preferences.

The Platform for Privacy Preferences Project (P3P) was developed by the World Wide Web Consortium (W3C), which oversees the web. Find out more about it from the W3C website, at:

http://www.w3.org/P3P/

The privacy features rely on a new system developed by the Platform for Privacy Preferences Project (P3P). It enables web sites to convert their privacy statements into a standard, computer-readable format. When you visit a web site, Internet Explorer reads its privacy statement, compares it to your settings and treats cookies accordingly.

1 To enter your preferences, go to Tools>Internet Options. Click the Privacy tab

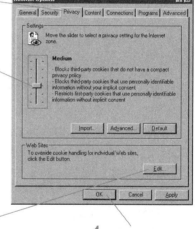

2 Move the slider to choose a privacy setting. Higher settings reduce the amount of data collected, but may mean web sites can't offer you personalised services

3 If you want to use a different setting for a site, click the Edit button and enter its address

4 Click OK

P3P is a new standard, so many sites haven't yet computerised their privacy statements. It'll be a while before everything works exactly as it ought.

5 If Internet Explorer rejects a cookie based on your settings, you'll see a privacy icon in the status bar. Double-click it for a report

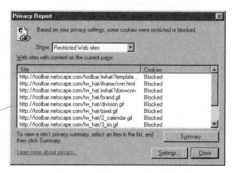

Pornography

Talk to someone who has never used the Internet, and they will almost certainly ask you about pornography. They might not know what the Internet is or how it works, but reading the papers has given them the impression that every other web page contains X-rated material – or worse.

Most adult sites have no desire to provide pornographic material to children. They usually have warnings on the front page and many require credit-card details as part of the registration process.

Truthfully, there is a lot of adult material on the Internet. Most of it is perfectly legal, although not to everyone's taste; some of it is deeply unpleasant and definitely illegal in this country. The global nature of the Internet, combined with the speed at which sites come and go, makes it almost impossible to eradicate illegal images. As for the rest, the problem is not so much that it is there, but that anyone can access it – including children.

If you have a family, you are probably concerned about the sort of material your children might encounter. At the same time, there are many excellent, child-friendly web sites. Preventing your children from accessing the Internet may protect them from inappropriate material, but it also cuts them off from all kinds of useful information.

There's no easy way to have the 'good' bits of the Internet without also enabling a computer-savvy child to find some of the 'bad' bits. However, there are several things you can do to minimise the risks. First, install the computer in a family room, so you can keep an eye on the screen, and don't let young children browse on their own. Second, make sure your children know that they shouldn't give out personal details, such as your address or phone number.

Internet Explorer has its own filtering system, the Content Advisor (find the controls under Tools>Internet Options> Content). However, it only works when web designers have added ratings to their pages, and most don't. You can't rely on it to protect your children.

Third, you can install filtering programs. These usually do two things: they prevent your children from accessing sites that appear on their blacklist, and they filter out pages containing forbidden words and phrases. Popular filtering programs include:

Cyber Patrol, from SurfControl, at:
`http://www.cyberpatrol.com/`

Net Nanny, from Net Nanny Software International, at:
`http://www.netnanny.com/`

Electronic mail

This chapter introduces Outlook Express, the e-mail program supplied with Internet Explorer. It shows you how to send and receive messages, add special formatting and attach files. It also explains how to keep track of addresses, sort and file your mail and set up e-mail accounts for all the family.

Covers

Chapter Eight

E-mail explained

E-mail is short for electronic mail, the Internet equivalent of letters and faxes. However, it's better than both of those, not only because it's quick and cheap, but also because you can attach files to an e-mail message. You can send text documents, pictures, sound samples and program files as well as simple messages.

You can send e-mail to anyone on the Internet; you just need to know their address, which will look something like:

johndoe@someplace.co.uk

The part before the @ is the recipient's user name

The part after the @ is the address of the recipient's Service Provider

When you send an e-mail message, it is delivered to the recipient's Service Provider very quickly – usually within a few minutes. It is stored in the recipient's mail box until he or she next logs on and checks for new e-mail.

E-mail is very efficient if you're dealing with someone who checks their mail box regularly, but not so good for getting messages to people who only log on once a week. It's handy for contacting people who are perpetually on the phone or out of the office and makes it easier to deal with people in different time zones. Instead of calling at an awkward hour, you can have a message waiting for them when they arrive at work.

You can also have news bulletins, reminders and other useful information delivered to your mail box. E-mail might not get as much media coverage as the web, but it's at least as useful and a lot less time-consuming.

Introducing Outlook Express

Outlook Express is a program for accessing e-mail and Usenet newsgroups (see Chapter 9). It has a few things in common with the Outlook application supplied with Microsoft Office, but don't get the two mixed up. Beneath the surface they are very different, and things that work in one won't necessarily work in the other. Outlook Express is optimised for sending mail over the Internet and is normally included with Internet Explorer.

You should also be able to run Outlook Express from Internet Explorer – click the Mail button and select Read Mail. If this doesn't work, go to Tools>Internet Options. Click the Programs tab and make sure 'E-mail:' is set to 'Outlook Express.'

1 To run Outlook Express, double-click its icon

Outlook Express

2 If you didn't fill in your e-mail details when you installed Internet Explorer, you'll be prompted to set up your account (see pages 21–22)

3 Outlook Express may connect to the Internet and check for new messages. Once it has finished, log off and click the Inbox icon

Outlook bar

Folder list – folders for all your messages

Folder bar – shows name of current folder

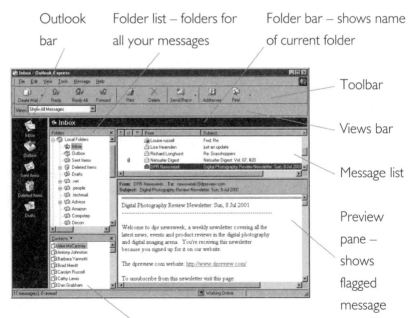

Toolbar

Views bar

Message list

Preview pane – shows flagged message

Contacts list – names from the Address book

Your Outlook Express window won't look exactly the same as the one on the previous page – you won't have as many folders or messages, and you may not see all the items. There are lots of different ways to organise this window.

1 Go to the View menu and select Layout

2 Select the items you want to display

3 Click Customize Toolbar to add or remove toolbar buttons, change the button size or hide the text labels

4 You can also change the relative sizes of most of the items by dragging the grey dividing bars

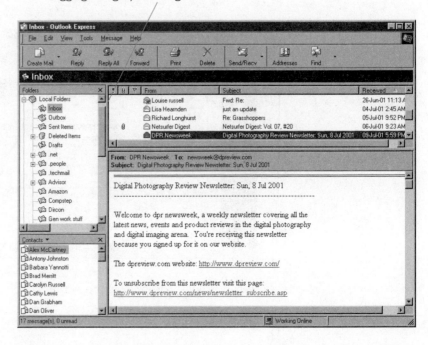

Sending e-mail

You have to be connected to the Internet to send a message, but you don't have to be on-line while you compose it. It's best to write your messages before you log on, then send them all in a batch. You can collect any new messages at the same time (see page 155).

1 To write a message, click the Create Mail button, select File>New>Mail Message or press Ctrl+N

The New Message window shown in Step 2 has a 'From:' line. This only appears when you have more than one e-mail account – see page 167.

2 A New Message window appears

3 Enter the e-mail address of the recipient

4 Fill in the 'Subject:' line

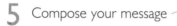

To send the same message to several people, enter all their addresses on the 'To:' line, separated by semicolons.

5 Compose your message

If you have one of the Microsoft Office applications, you can spell-check your message. When you've finished composing it, click the Spelling button, select Tools>Spelling or press F7.

6 Click the Send button, select File>Send Message or press Alt+S. This doesn't actually send the message, it just transfers it to the Outbox

7 When you're ready to send all your messages, click Send/Receive or press Ctrl+M. Outlook Express connects to the Internet and sends everything in your Outbox

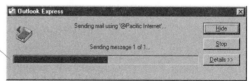

Formatted e-mail

Outlook Express enables you to use HTML commands to produce e-mail messages that look as good as web pages.

To specify which setting should be used by default, go to Tools> Options and click the Send tab. Set the mail format to 'HTML' or 'Plain Text.'

1 Use the New Message window's Format menu to switch between Rich Text (HTML) and Plain Text. A formatting bar appears when Rich Text is selected

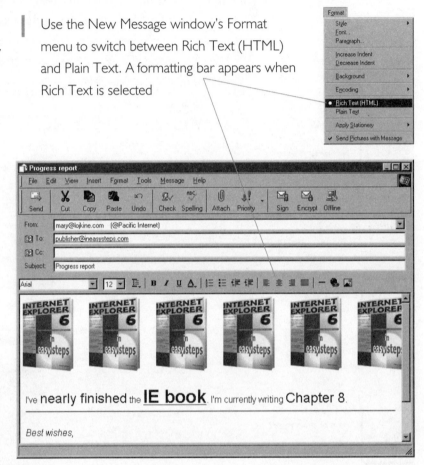

Stick to fonts that the other person will have: Arial, Comic Sans, Impact, Times New Roman and Verdana.

2 Use the drop-down lists and buttons to format your text. Use the Format menu to set the background colour and the Insert menu for lines or pictures

Formatted mail is fun, and handy when you're trying to catch someone's eye. However, it's only a good idea if you're sure the other person uses a program that can handle HTML mail. Formatted messages look awful in older e-mail programs and some people find them irritating. If in doubt, stick to Plain Text.

Stationery

Outlook Express comes with predesigned 'Stationery' that can add a touch of class to your correspondence or help you celebrate special occasions. As with formatted mail, Stationery is only a good idea if you're sure the recipient's e-mail program can display it.

 To specify a default Stationery design, go to Tools>Options. Click the Compose tab, select 'Mail:' and pick a design.

1 To compose a new message using Stationery, click the arrow next to the Create Mail button and select a design

2 Click Select Stationery for more choices – only a few of the designs are listed in the menu

 To design your own Stationery, go to Tools>Options and click the Compose tab. Click the Create New button to run the Stationery Wizard.
   There's also a Download More button that takes you to Microsoft's web site, where you'll find lot of extra designs.

3 Complete and send your message as usual

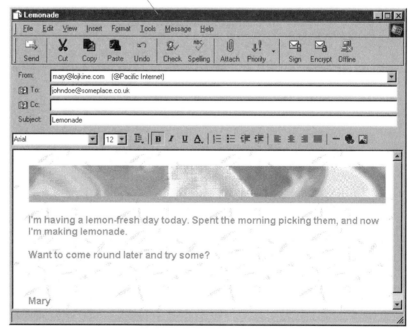

4 If you forget to select a Stationery design when you create your message, switch to Rich Text format (see the facing page), then select Format>Apply Stationery

Signatures

A signature is a short piece of text that is appended to the end of every message you send. If you're sending messages from work, it might include your contact details; otherwise you could use a personal comment or favourite quote. Keep it short, though – long ones soon become tiresome.

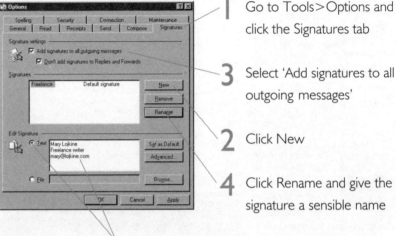

1 Go to Tools>Options and click the Signatures tab

3 Select 'Add signatures to all outgoing messages'

2 Click New

4 Click Rename and give the signature a sensible name

If you only want to sign some of your messages, don't select 'Add...' You'll be able to add the signature manually using Insert>Signature.

5 Select 'Text' and enter the text you want to add to your messages

6 Click Advanced if you have several accounts (see page 167) and only want to use this signature with some of them

You can create signatures for different moods or messages. Once you have more than one, it's best to sign messages manually – see above.

7 The text is added to the end of every message you create

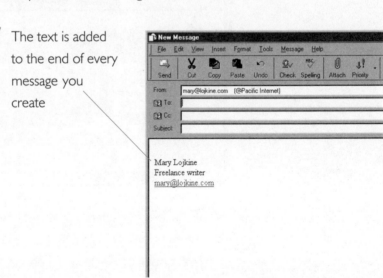

Receiving e-mail

Unlike 'real' mail, e-mail messages aren't automatically delivered to your door – or in this case, computer. When someone sends you an e-mail, it's delivered to your Service Provider's mail server, which puts it into your personal mail box. You must then log on and collect it.

1 To check your mail box, click Send/Receive. Outlook Express connects to the Internet (if necessary), sends any messages that are waiting in your Outbox and fetches any new mail. The new messages are placed in your Inbox. You can log off and read them in your own time

See page 165 to find out how to sort your incoming messages.

2 Select the Inbox folder to see the messages you have received

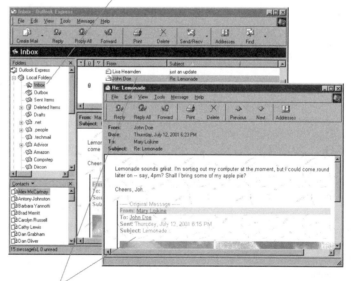

To print a message, click Print, select File>Print or press Ctrl+P.

3 Click once on a message to select it and display the text in the Preview pane at the bottom of the window, or twice to display it in a separate window

Replying and forwarding

It's easy to reply to an e-mail message, because Internet Explorer automatically adds the correct address.

1 To reply to a message, select it then click the Reply button. Alternatively, select Message>Reply to Sender or press Ctrl+R. Internet Explorer opens a New Message window

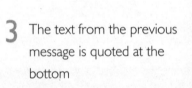

2 The 'To:' and 'Subject:' lines are already filled in

> If you're using the Plain Text format, the quoted section is marked with angled brackets:
>
> > Lemonade sounds great.
> > I'm sorting out my...

3 The text from the previous message is quoted at the bottom

4 Type your reply at the top

> Quoting is useful when you're dealing with people who receive a lot of mail. If you delete everything except the part of the message to which you're responding, it's easy for them to see what you're on about. However, you can turn this feature off if you find it a nuisance. Go to Tools>Options and click the Send tab. Deselect 'Include message in reply.'

5 Delete any superfluous material from the bottom section, then send the message as usual (see page 151)

Forwarding messages

You can also divert an e-mail message to a friend or to someone who is better able to respond to the sender.

1 To forward a message, select it and click the Forward button. Alternatively, select Message> Forward or press Ctrl+F. Enter the new address in the To: line

2 Add any comments you wish to make above the quoted text, then send the message

Attachments

You can e-mail pictures, document files and programs to your friends and colleagues. If you have a digital camera or microphone, you can bring your messages to life with snapshots or recordings. More prosaically, being able to exchange files by e-mail is handy if you're working from home.

1 Compose your message (see page 151) then click the Attach File button. Or select File Attachment from the New Message window's Insert menu

You can attach any kind of file, but don't send your friends large files without warning them first. You should also make sure they have the right software for viewing your files.

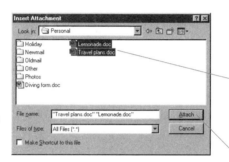

2 Find the file(s) you want to send – you can select several files at once by holding down Shift or Ctrl as you click

3 Click Attach

If you change your mind about one of the files, right-click on its entry in the 'Attach:' line, then select Remove from the pop-up menu.

4 The files are added to the message

5 Send the message in the usual way

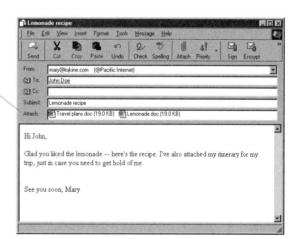

Receiving attachments

When you receive a message with attached files, you have two main choices: open the files, or save them onto your hard disk.

If you receive a file from someone you don't know, don't open it. The safest option is to delete the entire message. Alternatively, save the file on to your hard disk and check for viruses before you open it. This also applies to Word and Excel documents, which can carry macro viruses (see page 135).

1 If you see paperclip icons in the message list and preview pane, the associated message has one or more files attached. In some cases – for example, when a .gif or .jpg image has been attached – the file is displayed at the end of the text

2 When you open the message, the attached files are listed at the top. Right-click a file to open or save it

3 You can also deal with attached files by clicking the gold paperclip at the top of the Preview Pane. Click a file to open it, or click Save Attachments to save the files on to your hard disk

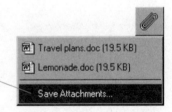

4 Click Browse and choose a folder

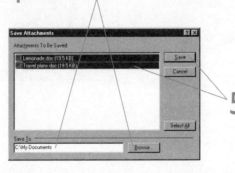

5 Select the files you want to save and click Save

Send and Receive options

Outlook Express' Options dialogue gives you control over when and how messages are sent and received.

Most of the options are fairly easy to understand. For more information, click the Help button ? in the top right corner of the dialogue box, then click an option.

1 Select Tools>Options. Click the General tab

2 Select '…at startup' if you want Outlook Express to connect and check for new messages as soon as you run it

3 Select '…every xx minutes' for Outlook Express to check again at regular intervals. You must also tell it what to do if you aren't on-line at that time

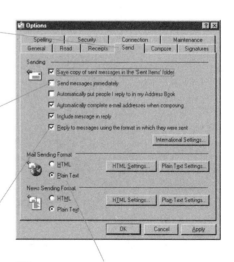

4 Click the Send tab

5 Select '…immediately' if you want Outlook Express to connect and dispatch each message as soon as you click the Send button (not usually a good idea)

6 It's courteous to reply to messages in the sender's preferred format

7 See page 152 for more on formatted mail

Address Book

The Address Book enables you to store all the e-mail addresses you use regularly. You can then add them to messages more easily.

1 To open the Address Book, click the Addresses button, select Tools>Address Book or press Ctrl+Shift+B

It's even easier to add the address of someone who has sent you an e-mail message. Select the message, then go to Tools>Add Sender to Address Book.

2 To add an address, click the New button and select New Contact. You can also select File>New Contact or press Ctrl+N

3 Fill in the person's name

4 Enter a nickname

5 Enter the e-mail address and click Add. Repeat if they have several

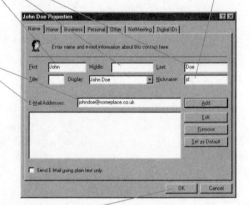

6 Click the Home, Business, Personal and Other tabs to add any extra information you wish to record

7 Click OK to finish

8 You can now enter the person's name or nickname in the 'To:' line of your messages. Outlook Express will look up the address when you send the message. Alternatively, double-click the person's entry in the Contacts list to create a pre-addressed message form

Finding addresses

If you don't know someone's e-mail address, the easiest way to find it out is by asking them. If that isn't practical, you may be able to track them down using one of the on-line directories. These are a lot like phone books (they are sometimes called 'White Pages'), except they contain e-mail addresses rather than phone numbers.

1 Go to Edit>Find>People

2 Choose an address service

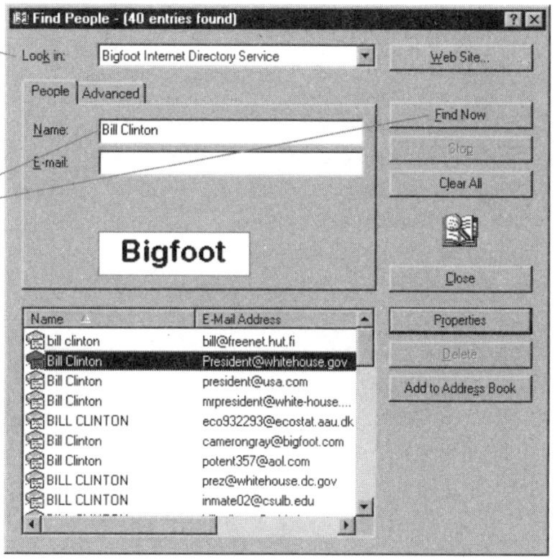

3 Enter the person's name and click Find Now

4 Outlook Express connects to the Internet, searches the database you selected and displays the bottom half of the dialogue box. With luck you'll see a list of names and be able to guess which address belongs to the person you are looking for

5 If you don't succeed, try one of the other services

6 You might also like to visit the web pages of the various services (just click the Web Site button) and register your details so your friends can look you up

Managing your e-mail

Initially you have five e-mail folders: Inbox, Outbox, Sent Items, Deleted Items and Drafts.

1 New e-mail is deposited in the Inbox (see page 155)

2 Outgoing e-mail waits in the Outbox (see page 151)

3 Once a message has been dispatched, it is moved to the Sent Items folder so you have a copy

The Deleted Items folder is like the Windows Recycle Bin – it stores items you think you won't need again until you're ready to get rid of them for good. To empty the folder, select Edit>Empty 'Deleted Items' Folder.

4 If you select a message and click Delete, select Edit> Delete, press Delete or press Ctrl+D, it ends up in the Deleted Items folder. You can rescue it if necessary

5 If you close a message without sending it, Outlook Express asks if you want to save it. Click OK to move it to the Drafts folder so you can work on it again later

Sorting your e-mail

As well as placing your e-mail in these folders, Outlook Express enables you to sort the messages in each one.

To change the categories, right-click on any of the tabs across the top and select Columns...

To sort your messages, click one of the grey category tabs at the top of the list. Click again to reverse the sort

Sorted by sender

Sorted by date received

Creating your own folders

Some messages can be thrown away as soon as you've read them, but there'll be others you want to keep. You can create additional e-mail folders and file them away tidily.

1. To create a new e-mail folder, go to File>Folder>New

2. Enter a name

3. To create a new top-level folder, select Local Folders. To make a subfolder, select one of your existing folders

4. Click OK to add the folder to the folder list

5. Use the mouse to drag messages into the new folder. Alternatively, select them (hold down Shift or Ctrl to select several at once), then go to Edit> Move to Folder. Select the folder and click OK

Finding messages

No matter how careful you are when you file your e-mail, there will come a day when you can't find the message where so-and-so said such-and-such. Outlook Express' Find function can usually track down the missing message – assuming it hasn't been permanently deleted.

1 To search for a message, go to Edit>Find>Message. Alternatively, press Ctrl+Shift+F

If you're reasonably certain that the message is in a particular folder, select it (rather than Local Folders) when you click the Browse button. The search will be restricted to that folder and Outlook Express should find the message more quickly.

2 Click the Browse button and select Local Folders to search everywhere. Make sure 'Include subfolders' is selected

3 Enter all the details you're sure about. Use the 'Message:' line for words that appeared in the text of the message

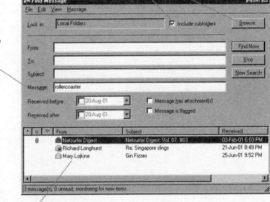

4 Click Find Now. Outlook Express searches for matching messages and lists them at the bottom of the box. Double-click a message to open it

5 If you get a long list of messages, enter more details and click Find Now again. Conversely, if you don't get any matches, try entering less information. A single, well-chosen word may be enough

6 Click New Search if you want to clear the dialogue box and start all over again

Message Rules

Message Rules enable you to sort your incoming messages by sender, subject or content and automatically highlight, file, delete or reply to them. They're useful for separating business and personal mail, or for blocking messages from people who keep sending you junk.

1 To create a Message Rule, go to Tools>Message Rules>Mail. Click the New button

You can select several conditions and actions at once to create very complex Rules. The dialogue boxes that enable you to specify the details of each condition usually have Options buttons that give you even more choices. For example, you can reverse the Rule so the action is applied when the message doesn't meet your condition.

2 Select a condition that the message must meet

3 Select the action to be taken

4 Click the blue, underlined text in the description to fill in details of the condition

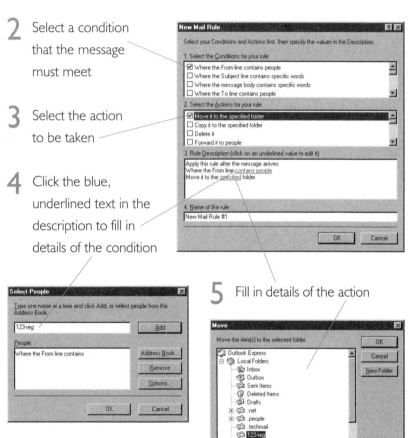

5 Fill in details of the action

6 Give the Rule a name and click OK

...cont'd

There are two easy ways to create Rules based on the sender of the message. Select a message from the correct person, then go to Message> Create Rule From Message to bring up the New Mail Rule box with the 'From' details already specified. Alternatively, you can ignore this person by selecting Messages>Block Sender.

7 All your Rules are listed in the Message Rules dialogue box

8 Use the checkboxes to enable or disable any of your Rules

9 Rules are applied in order. Click Move Up or Move Down to reshuffle them

10 Click a Rule to see its details

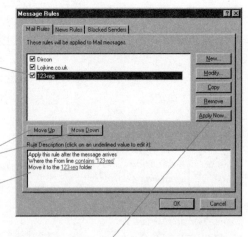

11 Click Apply Now to test your Rules

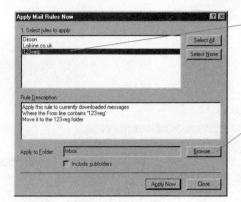

12 Select the Rule(s) you want to test

13 Click Browse to pick a folder – your Inbox is usually the best choice

14 Click Apply Now to proceed with the test

15 Close all the dialogue boxes and check whether your Rule has had the desired effect. If not, go back to the Message Rules dialogue box and select the Rule. Click Modify to change the condition and/or action

16 The active Rules (see Step 8) are applied to all your incoming mail

Multiple accounts

This section shows you how to set up Outlook Express to handle multiple accounts belonging to the same person. Page 169 explains how to manage accounts belonging to different people.

It's quite common to have more than one e-mail account. Many Service Providers give you several e-mail addresses, and the rise of free services has encouraged people to sign up for several Internet accounts. There's no point getting carried away, but it is useful to have separate addresses for business and personal mail.

1 To add a new account, select Tools>Accounts. Click Add and select Mail

2 The Internet Connection Wizard asks you questions about your account (see pages 21–22)

3 You'll end up back at the Internet Accounts dialogue box, with your new account added to the list

4 Select your main account and click Set as Default

Messages are dispatched from your default e-mail account unless you specify otherwise.

5 To change any of the details you entered in Step 2, select the account and click Properties

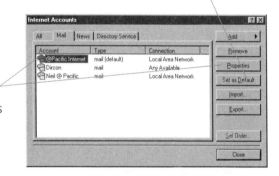

The 'Include this account...' option determines whether this account is checked when you click Send/Receive. If you only want to check it occasionally, deselect this checkbox.

6 The General section has your personal details. The name you enter here is the one people will see when you send them a message

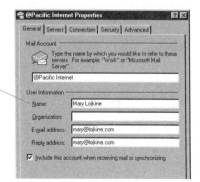

...cont'd

Outlook Express normally uses the default connection specified for Internet Explorer (see page 25), and that'll be fine if you only use one Service Provider. If, however, you have e-mail accounts with several Service Providers, you may have to specify the correct connection for each one.

7 The Connection section tells Outlook Express how to log on to the Internet when you click Send/Receive

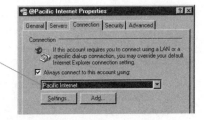

Using your accounts

You can send and receive mail from your default account in the usual way. Using secondary accounts is slightly more complicated.

1 If the 'Include this account...' option is selected (see 'Hot tip' on previous page), the secondary account is checked when you click Send and Receive. If not, you need to check it manually. Go to the Tools menu and select Send and Receive, then the name of the account

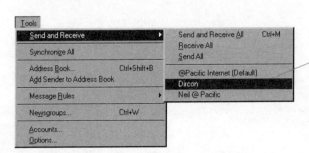

2 To send a message from a particular account, select it from the From: list at the top of the New Message form

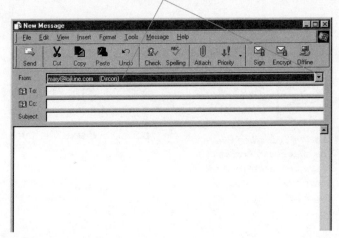

Identities

You can follow the instructions from the previous two pages to set up accounts for all the family, but everyone's mail will end up in a heap in the Inbox. A better solution is to create Identities for everyone. Each person can then have their own accounts, mail folders, Address Book and Message Rules. They can even change the layout of the Outlook Express window without affecting anyone else's interface. It's as if each person has their own copy of Outlook Express, except you only need to install the program once.

1   Go to File>Identities>Add New Identity

2   Type your name (or the name of the person who'll use this identity)

3   If you want to keep your mail private, select the 'Require a password' checkbox. Enter a password

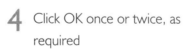

4   Click OK once or twice, as required

5   Click Yes to switch to the new Identity

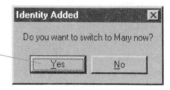

Use File>Import to transfer messages and Address Books from one Identity to another. You'll find your files in:

C:\Windows\Application Data\Microsoft

6   The Internet Connection Wizard appears so you can create an e-mail account for the new Identity (see pages 21–22)

Managing identities

Identities are straightforward. Once you've told Outlook Express who you are, it finds all your mail and sets things up the way you like them.

If the Folder bar is turned on (see pages 149–150 to find out how to activate it), it displays the name of the current Identity.

1 To choose the correct Identity, go to File>Switch Identities

2 Select a name, enter your password (if required) and click OK

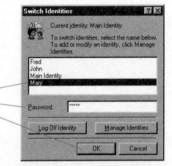

3 To determine what happens when you run Outlook Express, go to File> Identities>Manage Identities

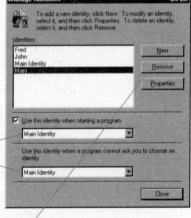

4 Select the start-up Identity. You can also set or change the identity to use by default

When you remove an Identity, all the mail that has been sent to that person is deleted.

5 You can also use the Manage Identities dialogue box to remove unwanted Identities. Select the identity you want to remove and click the Remove button

Hotmail

Hotmail is a free e-mail system owned by Microsoft. It's designed to be used from a web browser – the idea is that you can access your e-mail from any computer that's connected to the Internet, without having to set up an e-mail program. However, you can also download Hotmail messages into Outlook Express so you can read and respond to them off-line.

Although you can set up a new Hotmail account from within Outlook Express, it's better to go to Hotmail's web site at `http://www.hotmail.com/` You can then find out about the service before you choose your user name and password. Once that's done, configure Outlook Express to access your account.

1 Follow Steps 1 and 2 on page 167 to start the Internet Connection Wizard. Enter your name and Hotmail address

You can also tell Internet Explorer to use your Hotmail account when you click e-mail links on web pages. Go to Tools>Internet Options>Programs and set 'E-mail:' to 'Hotmail'.

2 When you're asked what type of server you use, select HTTP. Select Hotmail from the drop-down list that appears

3 When you finish, you'll be asked if you want to connect and download folders from the server. Click Yes

4 You can use your Hotmail account like any other e-mail account. However, it gets its own set of mail folders

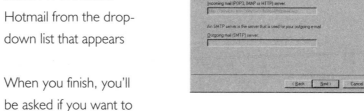

Making the most of e-mail

E-mail isn't just a way to bypass the postbox and fax machine. It also enables you to keep informed, join discussion groups, play games and have some fun with your friends.

The easiest way to fill your Inbox is by subscribing to mailing lists. There are two sorts: announcement lists that deliver regular newsletter-style messages, and discussion lists that are more like e-mail conversations. Everyone on the list submits their news, thoughts, recipes or whatever to the mail server, which copies them to all the members. They're a good way to get in touch with Internet users who share your interests.

Many of the bigger web sites have announcement lists that tell you what has been added each week. You can usually sign up somewhere on the site – in fact, you'll often find that registering (see page 108) puts you on the list. Discussion lists may also have associated web pages, but you usually sign up by e-mail. Get started by visiting the Topica website, which catalogues thousands of mailing lists. Find it at:
http://www.topica.com/

Play-by-e-mail games are also popular. You can get involved in everything from board, strategy and role-playing games to fantasy sports leagues. Some games work entirely by e-mail – you submit your move and wait for a response – while others take moves by e-mail, then display the results on a website.

Finally, there are lots of websites that use e-mail to deliver useful or amusing services. You can:

• send electronic postcards to your friends

• use automatic letter writers to generate romantic or sarcastic messages

• order a (picture of) a pizza over the web

On a more practical note, you can sign up for reminder services that send you messages on (or just before) important dates such as birthdays and anniversaries. Go to Yahoo! (see page 76) and search for 'e-mail' or 'cards' to find out what's available.

Usenet newsgroups

Usenet newsgroups enable you to communicate with Internet users who share your interests. This chapter shows you how to read and post messages, then explains newsgroup etiquette and customs.

Covers

Chapter Nine

Newsgroups explained

The Usenet newsgroups are the Internet equivalent of your local pub or social club. They aren't as pretty as the web, but they're interactive. If you're looking for gossip, trivia, advice, arguments and – very occasionally – news, Usenet is the place to find it.

Newsgroup messages are also referred to as 'posts' and 'articles'. The three terms are interchangeable.

You can think of a newsgroup as a public mail box for messages on a particular topic. Anyone can post a comment, and anyone else can read it and upload a reply.

Unlike web pages, newsgroups aren't stored in any particular place. All the messages are copied from one news server to the next, enabling you to access them locally. Rather than connecting to lots of sites from all over the globe, you download the latest messages from your Service Provider's news server.

There are over 50,000 newsgroups, although some Service Providers only carry the more popular ones. Some have a close-knit community of regular posters; others are larger and more anonymous. Either way, there's certain to be someone who wants to share your experiences, answer your questions, ask for advice or just pass the time of day.

Understanding newsgroup names

Newsgroup addresses look like:

`rec.arts.movies.reviews`

or sometimes:

`news:rec.arts.movies.reviews`

Newsgroups are organised hierarchically: each section of the address (moving from left to right) reduces the scope of the group. In this case `rec` stands for recreation, `arts` and `movies` are self-evident and the group only carries `reviews`. There are a dozen other `movies` groups, about 130 other `arts` groups, and over 800 `rec` groups in total.

`rec` is only one of dozens of top-level categories. However, you can find almost everything you're likely to want in `alt`, `comp`, `news`, `rec`, `sci`, `soc` and `uk`.

alt – alternative

Almost anyone can create an `alt` newsgroup, so the `alt` hierarchy is one of the liveliest sections of Usenet. Some of the groups are pretty wild, but most are just odd – if you're interested in alien conspiracies, urban legends or breakfast cereal, `alt` has much to offer. It's also a nursery for new groups, some of which eventually graduate to the more respectable hierarchies.

comp – computing

The `comp` groups deal with everything from hardware and software to artificial intelligence and home automation.

news – Usenet

The `news` groups are for discussion about Usenet. They aren't terribly exciting, but `news.announce.newusers` has lots of information for beginners.

The name 'Usenet' is derived from 'User Network.' Usenet is a network of computers (news servers) that exchange news messages.

rec – recreation

The `rec` groups cover hobbies, sports, arts and music, and are the best place to start. They tend to be friendlier than the `alt` groups and it's easy to find your way around.

sci – science

The `sci` groups cover mathematics, physics, engineering, chemistry, biological science, medicine, psychology and philosophy – everything except computing, basically.

soc – social

The `soc` groups deal with social issues. The biggest subsection, `soc.culture`, has over 100 groups dedicated to different countries and cultures. Genealogy, history and religion are well represented and there are several support groups.

uk – United Kingdom

The uk groups are a microcosm of Usenet as a whole. The busiest groups are `uk.people.gothic` and `uk.jobs.offered`, but you'll also find an *Archers* group, assorted political groups and a selection of `rec` and `religion` groups.

Getting started

There are many similarities between sending e-mail and posting messages to newsgroups. You use Outlook Express for both, and many operations are identical. However, you will notice some changes in the menus when you switch from sending and receiving e-mail to reading news.

The first thing you need to do is find out the address of your Service Provider's news server and set up Outlook Express to connect to it.

1 Run Outlook Express and select Tools>Accounts. Click Add and select News

2 Enter your name and e-mail address (Outlook Express should copy these from your default e-mail account, so you'll probably just have to click Next to accept its suggestions)

3 Fill in the address of your Service Provider's news server. You don't normally have to log on to news servers

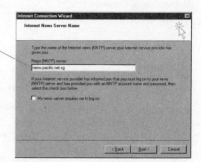

4 When you get back to the Internet Accounts dialogue box, click the News tab. You should see an entry for your news server. You may want to select Properties and give it a sensible name

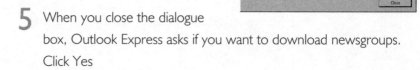

5 When you close the dialogue box, Outlook Express asks if you want to download newsgroups. Click Yes

6 Outlook Express downloads the names of the newsgroups carried by your Service Provider. This takes a few minutes, but you only have to do it once

7 The newsgroup list appears. You now need to select some newsgroups and 'subscribe' to them

Subscribing to a newsgroup isn't like subscribing to a magazine or joining a club. You don't have to pay, and you won't be added to a membership list. Subscribing just tells Outlook Express you're interested in a newsgroup – it's like making a Favorite for a web site.

8 Scroll down the list until you find a group that looks interesting, then select it and click the Subscribe button

9 To find groups covering a particular subject, type a word that might appear in the name into the 'Display...' box

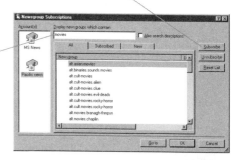

10 Click the Subscribed tab to see a list of the groups selected

11 If you want to add some more groups later on, select your news server from the Folders list. Click the Newsgroups button or select Tools>Newsgroups. You won't have to download the list again – Outlook Express stores it on your hard disk

Reading news

Reading newsgroup messages is slightly different from reading e-mail. Instead of downloading all the messages, which might take some time, Outlook Express only fetches the headers (the subject line, name of sender and so on). You then download the ones that sound interesting.

1 Select your news server from the Folder list to display your subscribed newsgroups

2 Double-click one of the groups to download the titles of the messages

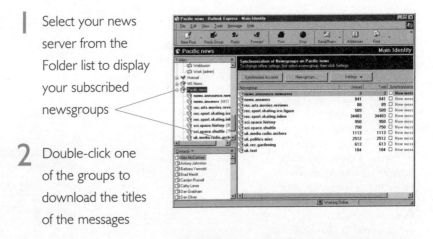

Some groups are very busy and receive hundreds of new messages each day. To tell Outlook Express how many headers to fetch, select Tools> Options and click the Read tab. Enter a number in the 'Get xx headers...' box.

3 Click a title to download and display the body of the message

4 On-going conversations are 'threaded' – the responses are displayed immediately below the original message. Click the plus ⊞ and minus ⊟ icons to expand and contract the threads

Posting messages

See page 184 before you start posting messages – there are lots of things that are considered rude on Usenet.

Posting messages is similar to sending e-mail (see page 151), but you address the message to the newsgroup.

If your response won't be of interest to anyone other than the original poster, e-mail it directly to them. Click Reply to Author, select Message>Reply to Sender or press Ctrl+R to create a pre-addressed form.

1 To create a new message, ensure you view the right newsgroup. Click New Post, select Message>New Message or press Ctrl+N

2 To respond to a message, select it. Click Reply to Group, select Message>Reply to Group or press Ctrl+G

3 Either way, Outlook Express launches a pre-addressed New Message window (if it's a response to an existing message, the original text is quoted – see p. 156). Fill in the Subject line and compose your message

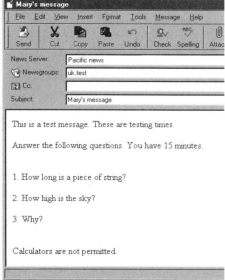

Want to practice? Post a message to the `alt.test` *or* `uk.test` *newsgroups. These groups were created for people who want to experiment with their software.*

4 Click Send, select File>Send Later or press Alt+S to transfer the message to your Outbox

5 Your message is uploaded to the news server when you click Send/Receive

Working off-line

To minimise the amount of time spent on-line, mark the messages you want to read and download them all at once. Then disconnect from the Internet and read messages off-line.

1 Select your news server from the Folder list

2 Select all your newsgroups, then click the Settings button and select Headers Only

News messages don't stay on the server forever; your Service Provider keeps clearing them out to make way for new ones. If a group is very busy, they may only be accessible for a day or two, so check popular groups regularly. You can also use Google Groups (see page 78) to read old posts.

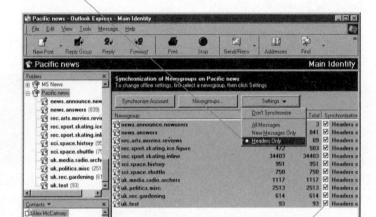

3 Deselect the checkboxes of any groups you don't want to bother with today

4 Click Synchronize Account. Outlook Express connects to the Internet and downloads the headers of any new messages sent to any of the selected groups

5 Log off and select Work Offline from the File menu

6 Double-click on one of your newsgroups. Scroll down the list of messages and select one that sounds interesting

7 Mark the message for downloading. To do this, go to Tools>Mark for Offline>Download Message Later. You can also mark an entire conversation (thread), or all the messages in the group

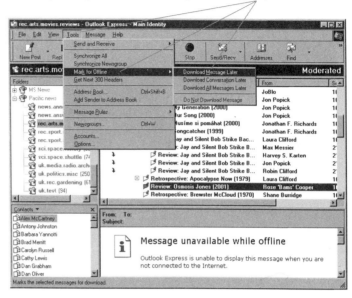

8 Mark all the other interesting messages, then repeat for the other newsgroups. Marked messages have blue arrows ⟍

9 When you've finished, select Tools>Synchronize All or go back to the list of groups and click the Synchronize Account button again

10 Outlook Express downloads the marked messages

11 Log off and select Work Offline again. Select a newsgroup, then select one of the messages you marked. You'll be able to display the message in the Preview Pane

Views

Outlook Express keeps newsgroup messages on your hard disk for the number of days specified under Tools>Options>Maintenance.

After a few days, you'll have downloaded lots of messages. Outlook Express displays the headers of the ones you haven't read in a bold font. Read messages are listed in a plain font so you can see the difference. Finding the new ones can still be a chore, though.

1   To make things easier, switch Views so only the messages you haven't read are displayed. To do this, go to View>Current View>Hide Read Messages

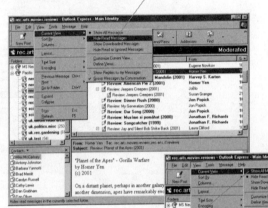

To see only the messages that can be read off-line, select View>Current View>Show Downloaded Messages.

2   To get the older messages back so you can see the new ones in context, select Show All Messages

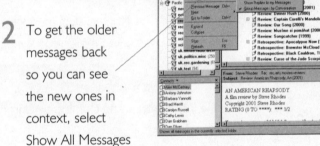

Turn on the Views bar (from View>Layout) for quick access to all the different Views.

3   You can also make boring conversations go away. Select the earliest message in the thread, then go to Message>Ignore Conversation

4   When you set the Current View to Hide Read or Ignored Messages, the entire conversation disappears, regardless of whether you've read the messages

Message Rules

Message Rules for newsgroups are much like Message Rules for e-mail (see page 165), except they're used to highlight or ignore messages, rather than to file them.

1 | Go to Tools>Message Rules>News and click the New button

2 | Choose the conditions. Usually you'll want to specify a newsgroup *and* select another condition

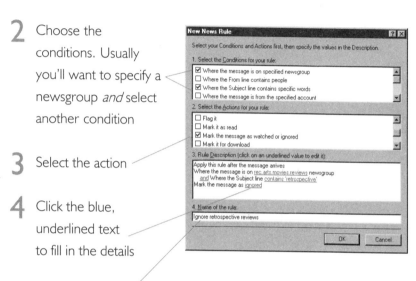

3 | Select the action

4 | Click the blue, underlined text to fill in the details

5 | Name the Rule

If you get fed up with an individual and want to ignore all of their messages, select one, then go to Message>Block Sender. Users of other programs call this 'kill-filing.'

6 | The Rule is applied to all the messages you receive from now on. This one has removed the 'retrospective' reviews of older films.

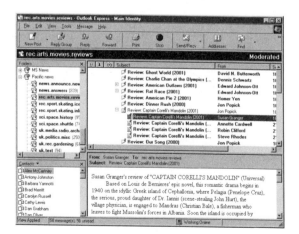

Netiquette

Usenet has a reputation for being hostile to beginners or 'newbies'. While it's true that some groups are hard to break into, most welcome anyone who displays a little common sense and courtesy. In particular, try to adhere to the following guidelines, known collectively as 'Netiquette'.

A 'flame' is an abusive message. Some groups tolerate and even encourage flaming; others expect members to be civil. If you post a flame, be prepared to get flamed back!

1   Always read the FAQ (see the facing page) before you start posting messages, to avoid (a) posting messages that are inappropriate and (b) asking questions that have already been answered hundreds of times.

2   Avoid posting the same message to several groups at once. This is known as 'cross posting', and it irritates the people who end up downloading your message several times.

3   Don't ever post the same message to lots and lots of newsgroups. This is known as 'spamming', and it irritates everyone. Sadly, you'll encounter lots of spam on Usenet, especially in the alt groups. Ignore it – responding just makes things worse.

4   Don't post Rich Text messages (see page 152), because most newsreading software won't display them properly. Stick to Plain Text.

For more advice on how to stay in line on-line, see 'Using the Internet in easy steps pocket', also published by Computer Step.

5   If you're replying to a message, don't quote more of the original than is necessary – most people won't want to read it all again. It's helpful to quote the sentence or two you're actually responding to, though.

6   Avoid posting messages that just say, 'Me too,' or, 'I agree.' Wait until you have something interesting to contribute.

7   Don't type your message in upper case. This is known as SHOUTING, AND IT MAKES YOUR MESSAGE DIFFICULT TO READ.

8   If you use a signature (see page 154), keep it short. Four lines is considered the maximum acceptable length.

FAQs

A FAQ is a compilation of Frequently Asked Questions – and their answers. FAQs exist for two reasons: to set out the group's scope and rules, and to answer all the questions a newcomer might ask.

'Lurkers' read the messages in a newsgroup, but don't post anything. It's a good way to find out what is acceptable in a particular group.

Most FAQs are posted regularly, generally weekly or monthly. If you 'lurk' in a newsgroup for a while, the FAQ should eventually appear. You can also find FAQs for many newsgroups in the Internet FAQ Archives at:

`http://www.faqs.org/faqs/`

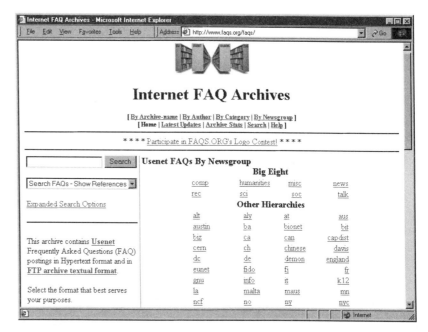

If all else fails, post a polite message asking someone to point you in the right direction. Some groups don't have FAQs; others have more than one, and some FAQs serve several groups. If you can't find a FAQ, lurk for a week or two to get a feel for the group.

Many FAQs represent the collective knowledge of the members of the newsgroup, and they can be fascinating reading in their own right. The question-and-answer format has also become popular elsewhere on the Internet – web sites often have FAQ pages.

Smileys and acronyms

Smileys and acronyms speed things up and help you clarify your comments.

Smileys

Smileys are also known as 'emoticons'. Don't use too many – some people think they're silly.

It's difficult to communicate your emotions in a brief text message to a stranger. This can lead to misunderstandings, particularly if you are prone to bluntness or sarcasm. Consequently, some people use 'smileys' – little faces made out of keyboard characters – to convey their state of mind.

There are many, many smileys. The three you're most likely to encounter are:

:-)	happy
;-)	winking or 'only joking'
:-(	sad or disappointed

(Turn the book through 90 degrees clockwise to see the faces.)

Acronyms

Common phrases are often abbreviated to their initials, producing TLAs (Three-Letter Acronyms) and ETLAs (Extended TLAs). You'll also see phonetic abbreviations.

Found an acronym that you can't decipher? Try the Acronym Finder, at (no spaces):

http://www.acronymfinder.com/

Common acronyms and abbreviations include:

AFAIK	As far as I know
B4	Before
BTW	By the way
F2F	Face to face
FYI	For your information
<g>	Grin
IMO	In my opinion
IMHO	In my humble opinion
IMNSHO	In my not so humble opinion
ISTM	It seems to me
ISTR	I seem to recall
IRL	In real life (meaning, off the Internet)
L8R	Later
ROFL	Rolling on floor laughing
RSN	Real soon now
RTFM	Read the 'flipping' manual

Index